LOOKING GOOD IN GOOD IN PRINT

LOOKING GOOD IN PRINT

A Guide to Basic Design for Desktop Publishing

Roger C. Parker

Ventana Press

Chapel Hill, NC

LOOKING GOOD IN PRINT:
A Guide to Basic Design for Desktop Publishing

Copyright © 1988 Roger C. Parker

Library of Congress Catalog No.: 87-051149

ISBN: 0-940087-05-7

Cover design and graphics by Suzanne Anderson-Carey, Berkeley, CA

Desktop publishing production by Laser Writing, Inc., Denver, CO, illustrations by LaserWriting, Inc., and Laser Press, Inc., Chapel Hill, NC

Linotronic output by National Teleprinting, Denver, CO

Copyediting by TechniProse, Inc., Chapel Hill, NC

First Edition, Fifth Printing

Printed in the United States of America

Ventana Press, Inc.
P.O. Box 2468
Chapel Hill, NC 27515
919/942-0220

Limits of Liability and Disclaimer of Warranty

The author and publisher of this book have used their best efforts in preparation of this book. These efforts include the development, research, and testing of the theories to determine their effectiveness. The author and publisher make no warranty of any kind, expressed or implied, with regard to the instructions and suggestions contained in this book.

The author and publisher shall not be liable in the event of incidental or consequential damages in connection with, or arising out of, the furnishing, performance, or use of instructions and/or claims of productivity gains.

Acknowledgments

The author and publisher wish to express appreciation to the following individuals who assisted in the production of this book:

Carolyn Bakamis
Edwin L. Bell
Tony Dopp
Scott W. Dunn
Trish Harmon
Lynn Jaluvka
Steve Lance
Brian Liptzin
Amy Rhue
Holly Russell
Teresa Smith
Mike Torcasso
Steve Valdeck
Mary Votta
William D. Wright

About the Author

Roger C. Parker is owner and president of The Write Word, Inc., *an advertising and marketing consulting firm based in Dover, New Hampshire. He is author of* The Aldus Guide to Basic Design *and* Using Aldus PageMaker. *His list of clients includes Apple Computer, Aldus, Hewlett-Packard, Microrim and Yamaha.*

The author may be reached at

The Write Word, Inc.
466 Central Avenue, #3
The Morrell Building
Dover, NH 03820
603-742-9673

Contents

Chapter 2: Tools of Organization

Chapter 3: Building Blocks of Graphic Design

Section Two: Putting Your Knowledge to Work

Chapter Six: Design Makeovers

Section Three: Getting Down to Business

Chapter 7: Developing a Format & Style

Chapter 8: Newsletters, Catalogs & Tabloids

Introduction

For many people using desktop publishing, graphic design is a mystery.

Until recently, graphic design was in the exclusive domain of art directors and design professionals whose very livelihoods depended upon creating professional, effective graphic images.

Desktop publishing has changed all that.

By eliminating the tedious instruments of graphic design (T-squares, rubber cement, etc.), desktop publishing has brought graphic design into the office and home. However, for many people using desktop publishing, graphic design is a mystery.

Looking Good in Print is a design book for users with little or no graphic design background who want to make the most of their desktop publishing investment. This design resource guide outlines the design skills necessary to create attractive, effective printed materials, such as newsletters, advertisements, brochures, manuals and other documents.

Regardless of your level of experience, you already may have more design skills than you suspect. In fact, you probably have an inherent, but as yet undeveloped sense of good design–often referred to as taste!

Consider, for example, how your experiences as a reader and consumer have given you valuable insights into the fundamentals of design:

- At a bookstore or newsstand, you're drawn to certain publications, while subconsciously avoiding others.

- Skimming through a newspaper, you read some advertisements, but ignore others.

- While watching television, you pay attention to some commercials, but use the remote control to avoid watching others.

Your inherent design skills help you screen effective messages.

This book teaches you how to consciously analyze your sense of design and translate it into creating effective, good-looking printed materials.

Effective Graphic Design—Luxury or Necessity?

Which is more important—the content of your message or the way your message looks?

The question is obviously a rhetorical one. Effective print communications depend on appearance as well as content.

From the simplest wall drawings of cave dwellers to the illuminated manuscripts of the Renaissance to yesterday's newspaper, history is rich with examples of the important role appearance has played in written communications. Gutenberg's invention of the printing press in the 15th century (and the subsequent design of decorative typefaces) only served to heighten the importance of good-looking print communications.

Today, effective graphic design is more important than ever. People are bombarded with print communications. Magazines and newspapers are more crowded with ads. Mailboxes are stuffed with catalogs, newsletters and other direct-mail solicitations.

Consequently, your message has a lot of competition, increasing the need for it to be as effective and appealing as possible.

In addition, because of the increasing complexity of products and services (coupled with recent changes in sales techniques), buying decisions are often based on brochures, proposals and other print communications rather than on direct hands-on, pre-purchase experience or person-to-person contact.

Effective Graphic Design Helps You Succeed

First impressions last. Effective graphic design favorably predisposes people to accept your product, service or point of view.

If your print communications fail to create a favorable first impression, the buying cycle may end before the actual virtues of your product or service are given further consideration. You never get a second chance to make a first impression.

Effective graphic design favorably predisposes people to accept your product, service or point of view.

Effective graphic design makes it easier for readers to understand your message. People often make acceptance and buying decisions based on their emotional and intuitive feelings about your product or service. Those feelings are highly influenced by the print communications used to describe them.

However, the opposite is also true.

Consider: Have you ever encountered a book you wanted to read, but just couldn't get into because of its poor graphic design? Perhaps the type was too small or the columns too wide. Even though it might have been a good read, the book was so poorly designed, it got in the way of your enjoyment.

The same thing happens every time a poorly designed newspaper ad or newsletter appears. Readers don't want to struggle through a poorly organized advertisement or publication. As a result, poor graphic design results in wasted money and lost sales opportunities.

Who Should Read Looking Good in Print?

Looking Good in Print is a design resource guide not for Madison Avenue art directors, but for individuals who are discovering the challenges and joys of desktop publishing, including

- Retailers, entrepreneurs and other professionals producing their own printed materials.

- Managers who need to improve the look of their materials.

- Writers who are producing their own finished artwork.

- Professionals interested in increasing the effectiveness of their brochures and newsletters.

In short, anyone who wants to improve the appearance and effectiveness of his or her desktop-published projects will find *Looking Good in Print* a lasting reference tool.

How to Use This Book

Looking Good in Print is organized into three sections.

- Section One, "The Elements of Design," outlines basic building blocks of graphic design and the underlying principles of effective design.

- Section Two, "Putting Your Knowledge to Work," demonstrates how the communicating power of a variety of different projects can be enhanced by simply rearranging the building blocks in more effective ways.

- In the final section, "Getting Down to Business," readers will learn to apply the basic tools of graphic design to specific projects they're likely to undertake as they put their desktop publishing hardware and software to work in the real world.

Poor graphic design results in wasted money and lost sales opportunities.

People new to desktop publishing should read the book from beginning to end, with particular emphasis on Section One.

Intermediate and advanced users can probably skip Section One, but will gain valuable insights from the remaining two sections.

For those who want further material on the subject, an extensive and carefully researched bibliography contains outstanding ancillary reading material on graphic design, typography, printing, production and related subjects.

How Well Should You Know Desktop Publishing?

This book assumes that you're already comfortable with your desktop publishing hardware and software. It assumes that your computer and printer are up and running, and you've gone through the tutorials which came with your software and are familiar with its basic commands.

The elements of good design are constant, regardless which hardware or software you use.

Looking Good in Print isn't a replacement for your software's documentation.

Please note that throughout this book, the terms *publication* and *document* are used to refer to any desktop publishing project regardless of its size or content. Thus a publication or document can be as small and simple as a business card or as large and complex as a book, newspaper insert or even a newspaper itself!

Hardware/Software Requirements

Looking Good in Print is a generic design guide. Whether you use an Apple Macintosh or an IBM PC/AT, Aldus PageMaker, Quark XPress, Ready-Set-Go, Ventura or any of the other fine desktop publishing or word processing programs available, this book will be a valuable resource. After all, the elements of good design are constant, regardless of your hardware and software!

All combinations of hardware and software are capable of producing excellent results—just as all combinations of hardware and software are capable of producing mediocre results. The difference lies not so much in your hardware and software, but in your willingness to embark upon a journey, to learn new concepts and to develop your inherent talents and abilities.

All combinations of hardware and software are capable of producing either excellent results or mediocre results.

About the Design of this Book

When producing *Looking Good in Print*, we were tempted to hire one of the nation's top graphic designers to format the pages and create an award-winning statement on contemporary design.

We resisted for two reasons. First, today's design trends often are tomorrow's rejects. More important, a book such as that would defeat the basic premise of *Looking Good in Print*—that high-quality results are attainable by anyone who wants to learn the basics of good design.

The examples featured throughout this book were produced in a simple, unembellished style. As your design and desktop publishing skills grow, you undoubtedly will produce far more elegant materials than those found in this book. We hope *Looking Good in Print* acts as a valuable stepping stone toward that end.

Let's get started.

Roger C. Parker
Golden, Colorado

SECTION ONE

The Elements of Graphic Design

Chapter 1: Beginning Observations

Part of the challenge of graphic design is that it has no universal rules.

Effective graphic design is based on knowing the building blocks of design and when to use them. Effective graphic design is also a matter of attitude, based on three important elements:

1. A willingness to experiment.
2. Confidence in your ability to develop the talent and know-how to do the job right.
3. Recognizing that effective graphic design is a "process," not an "event."

Part of the challenge of graphic design is that it has no "universal rules." It can't be reduced to a set of "if...then" statements. In graphic design, everything is relative. Tools and techniques that work in one situation won't necessarily work in another.

For example, it's impossible to define the amount of white space that should surround a headline or the correct typeface to use for your newsletter or book cover.

However, it's possible to summarize a few general observations about graphic design. They can provide a framework for applying the specific tools and techniques described later in this section. Before we discuss those important elements, let's take a look at the principles of successful graphic design.

Relevance

Everything in graphic design is relative to its particular communications function and unique graphic environment.

The more you define your project's purpose and environment, the better you'll do.

Just as in music, there's nothing right or wrong about notes such as Middle C or B-flat, there are no "good" typefaces or type sizes. There are only appropriately used typefaces and sizes.

Planning

Planning forms the basis of effective graphic design.

Before starting a project, ask yourself these questions:

1.   Who is the intended audience?
2.   What is the basic message you're trying to communicate?
3.   Where will readers encounter your publication?

    ❑ Newspaper   ❑ Magazine
    ❑ Mailbox   ❑ Point-of-sale
    ❑ Sales presentation   ❑ Other

4.   What similar messages have your readers encountered from your competitors?
5.   How does this publication relate to your firm's other publications?

The more you define your project's purpose and environment, the better you'll do.

The Role of Desktop Publishing

Remember that desktop publishing and graphic design are simply an extension of the organizing process that began when you started to write your project.

Desktop publishing works best as an extension of your writing, not as a last minute decoration.

To the extent that you can define your project's purpose and can prioritize the different parts of your message, you can create effective, good-looking print communications.

If, however, you're unclear about the purpose and undecided about the sequence and relative importance of the information you want to communicate, you're in dangerous waters. You're forced to operate subjectively rather than objectively.

For example, let's say you're laying out a magazine article which involves positioning a series of photographs. Unless you know how the photographs relate to the article, and which photograph is most important and which are merely supportive, there's no "right" or "wrong" way to organize them. Everyone's opinion would be equally valid. You're forced to be strictly subjective: "I think this photograph looks good here," etc.

If, however, you know how the photographs relate to the story and each other, it becomes relatively easy to decide which photograph should be largest, as well as the proper order and sizes for the other photographs.

Thus, desktop publishing and the tools of graphic design are simply an extension of your marketing and writing ability. Those design tools make it easy for you to add visual organization and emphasis.

Desktop publishing cannot compensate for a lack of initial planning or organization. Instead, desktop publishing and the tools of graphic design work best as an extension of your writing, not as last-minute decoration.

Coherence

Effective graphic design begins with a firm understanding of the goals and content of each project—be it an advertisement, brochure, newsletter or poster.

"Form" must always follow "function." Graphic design must be seen as a means of communication rather than mere decoration.

If you know the basic tools of graphic design and what you want to communicate, you'll be able to produce effective, good-looking publications.

"Art for art's sake" is definitely out. The appropriateness of each graphic element must be judged solely on its ability to help the reader quickly and easily understand your message.

"Pretension," or showing off the capabilities of your desktop publishing system, must not get in the way of communication.

Clarity, organization and simplicity are as important to graphic design as they are to writing.

Thus, always strive for coherence between appearance and content.

There should be a logical reason for the way you employ every graphic tool. That tool should relate to the idea it expresses as well as the environment in which the final product will appear.

Important ideas, for example, should be made visually more prominent than secondary ideas or supporting facts and figures.

YEAR-END SALE
Ends December 31

The idea of "coherence" should come as good news to those who've been intimidated by graphic design, thinking of it as an art practiced only by the blessed or the trained. This book is based on the assumption that if you know the basic tools of graphic design and what you want to communicate, you should be able to produce effective, good-looking publications.

Proportion

The size of all graphic elements should be determined by their relative importance and environment.

Because there are no absolutes in graphic design, success is determined by how well each piece of the puzzle relates to the pieces around it.

For example, proper headline size is determined by the amount of space that separates it from adjacent borders, text and artwork. A large headline in a small space looks "cramped."

I'M TOO CROWDED

Lorem ipsum dolor sit amet, con; minimim venami quis nostrud laboris nisi ut aliquip ex ea com dolor in reprehenderit in voluptate nonumy. Minimiami quis nostruiami quis nostruum veniami quisd laboris nisi ut aliquip ex ea com dolor in reprehenderit in voluptate nonumy. Minimiami quis nostruiami quis nostruum

veniami quis nostrud d laboris nisi ut aliquip ex ea com dolor in reprehenderit in voluptate nonumy. Minimiami quis nostruiami quis nostruum veniami quis nostrud d laboris nisi ut aliquip ex ea com dolor in reprehenderit in voluptate nonumy. Minimiami quis nostruiami quis nostruum veniami quis nostrud nostrud laboris nisi ut

Because there are no absolutes in graphic design, success is determined by how well each piece of the puzzle relates to the pieces around it.

Likewise, a small headline in a large space looks "lost."

NOBODY IS PAYING

ATTENTION TO ME

Lorem ipsum dolor sit amet, con; minimim venami quis nostrud laboris nisi ut aliquip ex ea com dolor in reprehenderit in voluptate nonumy. Minimiami quis nostruiami quis nostruum veniami quisd laboris nisi ut aliquip ex ea com dolor in reprehenderit in voluptate nonumy. Minimiami quis nostruiami quis nostruum

veniami quis nostrud d laboris nisi ut aliquip ex ea com dolor in reprehenderit in voluptate nonumy. Minimiami quis nostruiami quis nostruum veniami quis nostrud d laboris nisi ut aliquip ex ea com dolor in reprehenderit in voluptate nonumy. Minimiami quis nostruiami quis nostruum veniami quis nostrud nostrud laboris nisi ut

The proper thickness of lines—called rules—should be determined by the size of the surrounding white space and type.

If the lines are too thick, they interfere with reading.

I Feel I'm Being Overwhelmed

If they're too thin, they lack effectiveness.

WAR DECLARED!

Likewise, type size and the distance between lines should properly relate to the column widths that organize the type.

As you'll see later, wide columns are generally preferable for large type. Narrow columns are appropriate for small type.

Direction

Effective graphic design guides the reader through your publication.

Readers should encounter a logical sequence of events as they encounter and read your advertisement or publication. Graphic design should provide a road map that guides your readers from point to point.

The design of that map should follow the readers' natural tendency to read an advertisement or publication from upper left to lower right.

Graphic design should provide a road map that guides readers from point to point.

New Small Car Stuns Detroit Auto-makers

Lorum ipsum dolor sit amet, con; minimim venami quis nostrud laboris nisi ut aliquip ex ea com dolor in reprehenderit in voluptate nonumy. Minimum veniami quis nostrud laboris nisi ut aliquip ex ea com dolor in reprehenderit in voluptate nonumy.

Lorum ipsum dolor sit amet, con; minimim venami quis nostrud laboris nisi ut aliquip ex ea com dolor in reprehenderit in voluptate nonumy.

Lorum ipsum dolor sit amet, con; minimim venami quis nostrud laboris nisi ut aliquip ex ea com dolor in reprehenderit

in voluptate nonumy. Minimum veniami quis nostrud laboris nsum dolor sit amet, con; minimim venami quis nostrud laboris nisi ut aliquip ex ea com dolor in reprehenderit in voluptate nonumy. Minimum veniami quis nostrud laboris nisi erit in voluptate nonumy. Minimum veniami quis nostrud laboris nsum dolor sit amet, con; minimim venami quis nostrud laboris nisi ut aliquip ex ea com dolor in reprehenderit in voluptate nonumy.

LOGO

A Willingness to Experiment

"How do graphic designers work?"

Let's dispel the myth that design solutions appear like magic in a burst of creative energy or like a light bulb illuminating over the head of a cartoon character. Successful graphic design usually emerges from trial-and-error experimentation. Complicated solutions are the result of a willingness to try various design alternatives until the solution "looks right."

Effective desktop design is a process rather than an event.

Traditionally, graphic artists have used layers of tissue paper, soft pencils and big erasers. Tissue paper is used to trace successful ideas, which then can be used over again as the design project progresses. As the discard pile and eraser dust build up, the design solution gradually appears. Desktop publishing doesn't eliminate that trial-and-error process, but speeds it up by letting you try various arrangements of type and artwork on your computer screen.

Adventure

View your quest for more effective design techniques as a challenge.

Begin with an understanding that effective desktop design is a "process" rather than an "event." You're not going to wake up one morning a desktop design expert, nor is it likely you'll start a project and immediately come up with the solution.

Successful graphic design usually emerges from trial-and-error experimentation.

Effective design is a process of experimenting with the tools at your disposal and refining your solutions until they come quicker and with less effort.

In addition, begin your quest for effective desktop design as though you're embarking on a competitive exercise in which there are no "winners" or "losers," but rather "better" and "improved" solutions.

If there were universal rules, every ad, book, brochure, newsletter and poster would look the same.

Your initial goal is to improve the appearance and readability of your publications, not compete with Madison Avenue art directors.

Always remember: there's no single design solution suitable for every advertisement, brochure, newsletter or poster.

There are always "better" solutions, but never a "best" solution.

If there were universal rules, computer programs would replace graphic artists—and every advertisement, book, brochure, newsletter and poster would look the same. The resulting uniformity would rob the world of the diversity and visual excitement that add so much to magazines, newspapers and even our daily mail!

Surprise Versus Boredom

Avoid boring your readers.

One of your biggest challenges as a desktop designer is to reconcile the continuing conflict between consistency and "surprise." Your goal is to create advertisements and publications that are consistent within themselves, without being boring. Boredom occurs when predictability and symmetry become too obvious.

Boredom occurs when predictability and symmetry become obvious.

Thus, your publications should be consistent within themselves and with your firm's other print communications, yet they should be visually distinct. If you use one-inch margins in Chapter One, you should use one-inch margins in Chapter Ten—unless there are compelling reasons for change (e.g., Chapter Ten has large photographs, etc.).

Page-to-page consistency can be provided in any of the following ways:

- Use the same margins.
- Use identical typeface, type size and line spacing for body copy, headlines, subheads and captions.

- Use uniform paragraph indents and spaces between columns and around photographs.
- Repeat the same graphic elements on each page, such as using vertical lines, columns or borders of the same width.

For example, you can create an "artificial horizon" by using a strong line or graphic element repeated on each page throughout your publication.

High-impact, easy-to-read publications tend to have a lot of contrast.

Contrast

Contrast enhances the communicating power of your publication.

Contrast refers to the "color" of your publication, as determined by the relative amount of space devoted to text, artwork and white space. When analyzing a publication, compare "dark" areas—such as large, bold headlines, dark photographs or blocks of body copy—and notice how they're offset by lighter areas with little type.

High-impact publications tend to have a lot of contrast. Each page or two-page spread has definite "light" and "dark" areas, with lots of white space and illustrations.

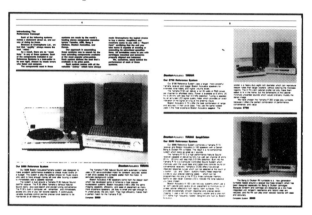

Contrast enhances the communicating power of your publication.

You can create publications low in contrast, where all pages and parts of pages are a uniform shade of "gray." Formal reports, policy statements and press releases often are low in contrast.

Contrast can be observed by turning the publication upside down. Viewed from that perspective, your eyes aren't misled by the tendency to read individual words. Instead, you concentrate on the overall "color" of the publication.

Uniformity Versus Consistency

Use contrasting sizes to create tension.

Tension is healthy. It keeps the reader interested. Uniformity leads to boredom.

Effective graphic design is based on developing consistent ways of handling diversity. Your designs must be dynamic enough to keep the reader interested, yet consistent enough so that your advertisement or publication emerges with a strong identity.

Consistency is a matter of detail. It involves using restraint in choosing typefaces and type sizes, and using the same spacing throughout your document.

Consistency leads to style. Style reflects the way you handle problems that come up again and again. It's not something you have from the beginning. Rather, it emerges as you develop your desktop publishing design skills.

Unity

Always provide a single dominant visual to capture the reader's attention.

The single dominant visual helps organize the reader's eye-movement throughout your publication, in addition to communicating relative importance.

Tension keeps the reader interested. Uniformity leads to boredom.

For example, consider a page with four equal-sized photographs.
That puzzles the reader: "Which photo should I look at first?"
The reader can't determine which photograph is most important.
Hence, the message is weakened.

When one photograph is larger, however, not only is the page more interesting, it sends the reader a nonverbal message to pay more attention to the big photograph than the others. The message is reinforced by its visual presentation.

Your job is to assemble a total picture from a series of parts.

Never Lose Sight of the Total Picture

Think of graphic design as the visual equivalent of a jigsaw puzzle.

Your job is to assemble a total picture from a series of individual parts. No piece of the puzzle should be isolated from the others. The various parts must fit together harmoniously.

The "total picture" includes consideration of the environment in which your advertisement or publication will be distributed.

For example, when designing a newspaper advertisement, consider how it will look when surrounded by editorial materials and other advertisements.

When planning a newsletter or direct-mail piece, imagine how it will look when it arrives in the recipient's mailbox.

When planning a magazine cover, consider how it will look surrounded by other magazines on the newsstand.

When creating product literature, consider how it will appear when placed in a literature rack.

Consistency

When working on multi-page publications, such as newsletters, brochures or books, work on two-page spreads instead of individual pages.

If you concentrate on each page as though it were a self-contained entity, you might end up creating two pages that look good individually, but don't work side by side.

This left-hand page is an attractive, self-contained visual unit.

If you retain each page as a self-contained entity, you might end up creating pages that look good individually, but don't work side by side.

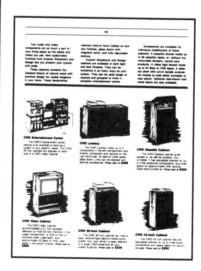

This right-hand page also works as an attractive, self-contained visual unit.

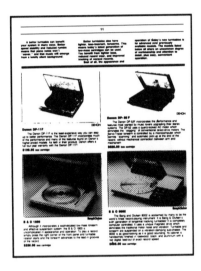

When viewed side by side, however, they "fight" each other and present a disorganized, difficult-to-read image.

Unless designed side by side, pages can "fight" each other and present a disorganized, difficult-to-read image.

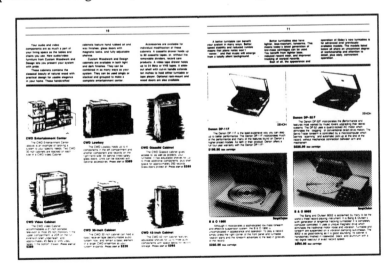

Remember that readers seldom encounter individual pages. Left- and right-hand pages usually are viewed together.

Restraint

Discipline yourself to practice restraint.

Restraint is probably the most difficult design principle to apply in a consistent manner. That's because desktop publishing presents you with tremendous design power—power which just a few years ago was limited to those who had years of training and tens of thousands of dollars worth of equipment.

With so much power at your fingertips, it's easy to forget that straightforward simplicity is a virtue and that graphic design should be invisible to the reader.

Restraint is the most difficult design principle to apply in a consistent manner.

Restraint is exemplified by restricting changes in typeface and type size to an absolute minimum.

In making design decisions, consider the degree to which design enhances the basic message you want to communicate.

Like the boy who cried "Wolf!" too often, unnecessary emphasis weakens your publication.

Remember that emphasis only can occur when contrasted against a stable framework. Like the boy who cried "Wolf!" too often, unnecessary emphasis weakens your publication to the point where it loses all impact.

Next, let's examine the tools available to you as you plan and create advertisements or publications.

Chapter 2: Tools of Organization

Effective graphic design uses a variety of organizational tools to help readers quickly and easily understand your message.

The primary purpose of graphic design tools is to guide readers' eyes from one point to another. The secondary purpose is to keep readers informed of their progress and help them quickly locate desired information. Two types of organizers are *graphic* and *text*. However, the distinction between them often is blurred.

Graphic Organizers

Graphic organizers are those created by your desktop publishing program's drawing tools.

Different desktop publishing programs offer different ways of implementing those tools. These include...

Grids

Use grids to organize your advertisement or publication. Grids define the horizontal and vertical placement of type and artwork.

Grids consist of nonprinted lines that show up on your computer but not on your printed material.

Grids are particularly valuable in designing advertisements, because they help you avoid reinventing the wheel each time you create an ad.

Grids determine the horizontal placement of columns, and the vertical placement of headlines, body copy and artwork.

For example, grids help determine where headlines and body copy are placed on a page. Grids also determine how far up from the bottom of a page columns end.

Grids help you avoid reinventing the wheel each time you create an ad.

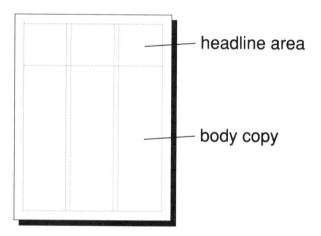

headline area

body copy

Desktop publishing programs differ in their ability to create grids. Some programs provide you with ready-made grids, which can be modified by adjusting the height and width of the boxes, as well as the spaces between them.

Others separate column creation from horizontal guidelines. All programs, however, let you establish formats that will be automatically maintained from page to page.

Borders

Use borders to isolate a document from its environment.

Borders work with white space to determine publication "color" and emotional "tone." Borders can be tangible or assumed.

Tangible borders are lines that outline an advertisement or publication. Assumed borders are created by the readers' eyes as they encounter the edges of columns of type or artwork.

The basic border consists of a large box drawn around all four sides of a publication. With most desktop publishing programs, the easiest way to create one is to use the box-drawing tool. Either single or double lines, thick or thin, can be used.

All four borders don't have to be the same, however. Different borders can be used at the top, bottom and sides of a publication.

Borders determine "color" and emotional "tone."

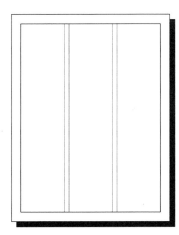
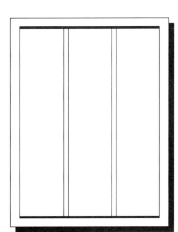

Borders don't have to extend the full height or width of a publication.

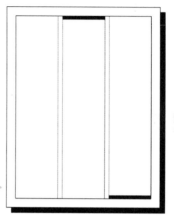

Sometimes, side borders are omitted. In those instances, page borders are created by columns of type or artwork.

Type and artwork can form borders.

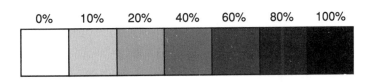

Thick borders can be created by using the box-drawing tool and filling the boxes with solid (100 percent) black or shades of gray.

Allow "breathing room" between the borders and type or artwork.

Margins

Margins determine the relationship of columns to borders.

Margins determine the distance between the boundaries of a page and the advertisement or publication's "live area"—the space where type, artwork and organizers, such as page numbers or borders, appear.

There always should be "breathing room" between the borders and type or artwork.

The more space, the "lighter" the publication. Thinner margins result in "darker" publications.

Rules

Rules are lines used to separate one part of a publication from another.

Rules can be horizontal or vertical, thick or thin.

Vertical rules often are used to separate columns, particularly when nonjustified type is used.

Horizontal rules often separate topics within a column.

Use horizontal rules to separate topics within a column.

Horizontal rules often are used to draw attention to "pull-quotes" (short sentences that summarize the key points of an article).

This is a pull-quote. (See how it got your attention!)

Horizontal rules also are used to draw attention to subheads, which can be used to divide long blocks of text.

Choose rules that complement the "color" of your publication.

Thick rules "darken" a publication and are most effective when set off by white space.

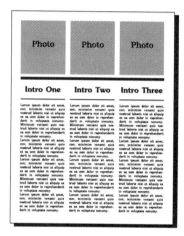

Thin rules are appropriate for publications with a lot of copy.

Thin rules are appropriate for publications containing a lot of copy.

Boxes

Use boxes to separate parts of a publication.

Boxes often are used for sidebars (self-contained articles that relate to longer, feature articles).

Use boxes to isolate information.

Boxes often are used to isolate publication information, such as addresses and phone numbers, or to give credit to the individuals responsible for producing a publication.

Boxes also are used to create coupons to generate reader response. Most desktop publishing programs allow you to create boxes with dashed borders to clearly identify the coupon.

Small rectangular or square boxes can be used to indicate the end of an article. ■

Columns

Use columns to organize the horizontal placement of type and artwork.

Type rarely extends in an unbroken line from the left side of your page to the right. Type usually is arranged in one or more *columns*—invisible, nonprinted lines that determine the placement and width of lines of type, illustrations or photographs.

Columns, and the distance between them, have a great deal of influence on publication "color."

Closely spaced columns "darken" an advertisement or publication. Closely spaced columns often make a publication more difficult to read, because the reader's eye tends to jump the gap between columns.

Closely spaced columns can make reading difficult.

Extra space between columns "lightens," or opens up, an advertisement or publication, and also clearly separates one column from another.

Column width determines line length. Line length influences publication readability. Remember that readers scan groups of words rather than individual letters. Wide columns are more difficult to read because the reader's eyes have to shift several times from left to right when reading each line. In addition, at the end of each line, the reader's eyes have to jump down to the left to find the beginning of the next line.

Line length influences publication readability.

8 point text placed on a 24 pica column is very difficult to read. 8 point text placed on a 24 pica column is very difficult to read.8 point text placed on a 24 pica column is very difficult to read.8 point text placed on a 24 pica column is very difficult to read. 8 point text placed on a 24 pica column is very difficult to read. 8 point text placed on a 24 pica column is very difficult to read.8 point text placed on a 24 pica column is very difficult to read.8 point text placed on a 24 pica column is very difficult to read.

The wider the column, the more difficult it is for the reader's eyes to make a smooth transition from the end of one line to the beginning of the next without getting lost.

Column width should be determined by type size. Thus, use narrow columns for small type sizes.

But 8 point text in a 12 pica column is readable. But 8 point text in a 12 pica column is readable. But 8 point text in a 12 pica column is readable. But 8 point text in a 12 pica column is readable. But 8 point text in a 12

Use wider columns for larger type sizes.

12 point type looks good when placed in 24 pica columns. 12 point type looks good when placed in 24 pica columns. 12 point type looks good when placed in 24 pica columns. 12 point type looks good when placed in 24 pica columns.

Remember that all columns on a page don't have to be the same width. Good-looking publications can be created by using a variety of column widths.

Good-looking publications can be created by using a variety of column widths.

For example, subheads and illustrations can be laid out side by side in a narrow column adjacent to one or more wide columns.

Type and artwork can extend across one or more columns. For example, type and artwork arranged in a five-column format can be organized in the following ways:

Type can be arranged a number of ways on a five-column grid.

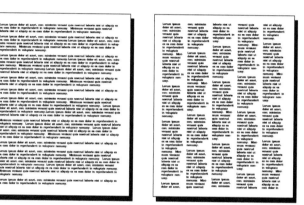

One wide column

Five narrow columns

One narrow column, two wide columns

One double column, one triple column

Variations on the above are permissible within a document. Column widths can be changed for different sections of a publication or even different parts of a page. Type and artwork should always be lined up with the invisible column guides.

A two-column photograph or illustration, "A," on a five-column grid looks good when edges of the photograph are aligned with column guides.

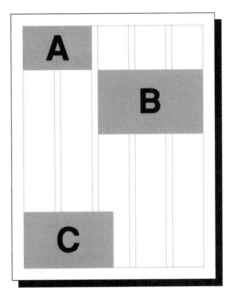

Likewise, a three-column photograph, "B," on a five-column grid looks good when the edges of the photograph are lined up with the column guides.

But, a two-and-a-half column photograph, "C,"on a five-column grid creates unsightly "half columns" of white space or short columns of type.

Text Organizers

Letters, words and numbers can be used to organize your advertisement or publication.

Those organizational tools help readers understand your message quickly and easily.

Headlines

Use headlines to invite readers to become involved in your advertisement or articles in your publication.

Headlines are the basic text organizing tool. Headlines help readers decide whether to read an advertisement or an article.

Headlines should be as short and concise as possible so their meaning can be understood quickly.

They should be clearly differentiated from body copy, which can be done in two ways.

Set off headlines by using a contrasting typeface.

Headlines are the basic text organizing tool.

This Headline Is Set in Helvetica

However, the copy is set in Times Roman. However, the copy is set in Times Roman. However, the copy is set in Times Roman. However, the copy is set in Times Roman. However, the copy is set in Times Roman. However, the copy is set in Times Roman. However, the copy is set in Times Roman. However, the copy is set in Times Roman. However, the copy is set in Times Roman. However, the copy is set in Times Roman. However, the copy is set in Times Roman. However, the copy is set in Times Roman. However, the copy is set in Times Roman. However, the copy is set in Times Roman. However, the copy is set in Times Roman. However, the copy is set in Times Roman. However, the copy is set in Times Roman. However, the copy is set in Times Roman.

Times Roman. However, the copy is set in Times Roman. However, the copy is set in Times Roman. However, the copy is set in Times Roman. However, the copy is set in Times Roman. However, the copy is set in Times Roman. However, the copy is set in Times Roman. However, the copy is set in Times Roman. However, the copy is set in Times Roman. However, the copy is set in Times Roman. However, the copy is set in Times Roman. However, the copy is set in Times Roman. However, the copy is set in Times Roman. However, the copy is set in Times Roman. However, the copy is set in Times Roman. However, the copy is set

For example, headlines set in sans-serif type (discussed on pp. 49-50) often are used with body copy set in a serif typeface—the technique most often used for documents such as advertisements, books, brochures and newsletters.

Alternately, emphasize headlines by using the same typeface in a larger size or heavier weight.

Add impact to headlines by using a contrasting typeface or larger type.

This Headline Is Set in Helvetica

So is this body copy, but it's set in a smaller size. So is this body copy, but it's set in a smaller size. So is this body copy, but it's set in a smaller size. So is this body copy, but it's set in a smaller size. So is this body copy, but it's set in a smaller size. So is this body copy, but it's set in a smaller size. So is this body copy, but it's set in a smaller size. So is this body copy, but it's set in a smaller size. So is this body copy, but it's set in a smaller size. So is this body copy, but it's set in a smaller size.

So is this body copy, but it's set in a smaller size. So is this body copy, but it's set in a smaller size. So is this body copy, but it's set in a smaller size. So is this body copy, but it's set in a smaller size. So is this body copy, but it's set in a smaller size. So is this body copy, but it's set in a smaller size.

So is this body copy, but it's set in a smaller size. So is this body copy, but it's set in a smaller size. So is this body copy,

but it's set in a smaller size. So is this body copy, but it's set in a smaller size. So is this body copy, but it's set in a smaller size. So is this body copy, but it's set in a smaller size. So is this body copy, but it's set in a smaller size. So is this body copy, but it's set in a smaller size. So is this body copy, but it's set in a smaller size. So is this body copy, but it's set in a smaller size. So is this body copy, but it's set in a smaller size. So is this body copy, but it's set in a smaller size. So is this body copy, but it's set in a smaller size.

So is this body copy, but it's set in a smaller size. So is this body copy, but it's set in a smaller size. So is this body copy, but it's set in a smaller size. So is this body copy, but it's set in a smaller size. So is this body copy, but it's set in a smaller size. So is this body copy, but it's set in a smaller size. So is this body copy, but it's set in a smaller size.So is this

The greater the difference between headline and body copy, the easier it is for readers to identify and read your headline.

Design your headlines for impact. But make them as easy to read as possible. There are several ways to accomplish that.

In general, avoid long headlines set in upper-case type.

LONG HEADLINES SET IN UPPER-CASE TYPE ARE HARDER TO READ

Avoid long head-lines set in upper-case type.

Headlines set in upper-case type occupy more space and slow readers down. Readers are unaccustomed to words set exclusively in upper-case type, which are difficult to view at a glance. In general, limit upper-case headlines to two or three words.

FIRE SALE!

Subheads

Subheads can be used to continue the organizing task that begins with headlines.

Subheads break up body copy into manageable segments, and improve appearance and enhance readership by providing a transition between headlines and body copy. They also provide visual contrast and identify the content of the body copy. They allow readers to quickly locate desired information.

Compare these two examples.

Subheads break up body copy and provide visual contrast.

Here, you're faced with a long expanse of type. Reading it is a chore, because the page is so "dark" and because you don't have a clue as to the contents of the page.

This example is more inviting because the page is more "open" and you easily can decide whether the body copy relates to your interests.

Subheads can be set apart from body copy by various techniques, including

Placement:

Subheads can be placed inside or next to the body copy.

Use placement, typeface, size, alignment or rules to draw attention to subheads.

Typeface:

Like headlines, subheads can be set in a typeface that contrasts with the body copy.

Size:

Subheads should be set in larger type than the body copy.

Alignment:

Subheads can be set centered, flush left or flush right.

Subhead style should be uniform throughout your publication.

Rules:

Subheads can be emphasized by horizontal rules above or below the words.

Uniformity is important. Subheads should be treated the same way throughout your advertisement or publication.

Captions

Use captions to relate photographs and illustrations to the rest of your publication.

Next to headlines, captions are the best-read part of a publication. Accordingly, use captions to summarize important points.

Captions can be placed in a variety of ways.

Lorum ipsum dolor sit amet, con; minimim venami quis nostrud laboris nisi ut aliquip ex ea com dolor in reprehenderit in voluptate nonumy.

Photo

Captions can be placed next to the artwork they describe.

Next to headlines, captions are the best-read part of a publication.

Captions can be placed above the artwork.

Lorum ipsum dolor sit amet, con; minimim venami quis nostrud laboris nisi ut aliquip ex ea com dolor in reprehenderit in voluptate nonumy.

Photo

Photo

Lorum ipsum dolor sit amet, con; minimim venami quis nostrud laboris nisi ut aliquip ex ea com dolor in reprehenderit in voluptate nonumy.

Captions also can be placed below the artwork.

Whether above or below the artwork, captions can extend the full width of the photograph or illustration, or they can be aligned with either the left- or right-hand edges.

Caption width should be in a pleasing proportion to the width of the photograph or illustration described, as well as surrounding white space and body copy.

Uniformity is important. Captions should be treated the same way throughout a publication. Thus, if you align captions with the left-hand edge of photographs on Page 5, align them with the left-hand edge of photographs on Page 20.

Masthead

Create a distinctive masthead for your publication.

A masthead is a distinctive type treatment of the title of your publication. It should remain the same from issue to issue. You should devote a great deal of time to designing the masthead.

Mastheads should be prominent enough to provide a quick and lasting visual identity.

Although they should be large and distinct enough to be recognizable at a glance, mastheads should not overshadow the headlines on the first page of each issue.

Logo

"Sign" your ads with your firm's logo.

Use your firm's logo as a "signature" on your document.

A logo is a distinctive visual treatment of your firm's name that projects an important image.

Logos reflect your firm's philosophy.

Often, the letter-spacing has been specially modified to create a distinct effect called a logo type.

A logo is a graphic symbol that relates to your firm's type of business.

EMPLOYEE BENEFIT PLANS
3644 Golden Years Drive•Malibu CA 92777
213 555-3333

This symbol also can reflect your firm's philosophy.

Logos should be large enough to be easily identified, yet they shouldn't overwhelm or detract from surrounding body copy or other information.

Logos are particularly important in magazine and newspaper advertisements. They not only provide immediate visual identification and ad-to-ad consistency, they also provide a strong conclusion for the ad.

Headers

Information at the top of each page should inform readers about the contents of that page.

The space at the top of each page in a newsletter or book should reinforce the identity of the publication, as well as serve as a road map to help readers locate specific information.

Publication title, chapter and section titles, and the author's name are frequently repeated at the top of each page.

Alternately, this space can be used to summarize the content on each page, helping readers quickly locate desired information (see above).

Footers

Information also can be placed at the bottom of each page.

Page numbers frequently appear at the bottom of each page, as do publication titles and bylines.

Symbols

Use asterisks, bullets and numbers to organize ideas in lists.

Use asterisks, bullets or square boxes when all items are equally important.

Ingredients of a healthy diet include representatives of all major food groups, including:

• Butter	• Milk
• Eggs	• Corn
• Meat	• Cereal
• Fish	• Pop Tarts

Organize lists with symbols and numbers.

Use letters or numbers to establish a priority of importance.

Bills to pay:

1) IRS
2) Home mortgage
3) Car payment
4) Credit card payment
5) Utilities
6) Medical insurance
7) Hobby shop
8) Florist

Jumplines

Use jumplines to inform readers when articles are continued from one page to another.

Lorum ipsum dolor sit amet, con; minimim venami quis nostrud laboris nisi ut aliquip ex ea com dolor in reprehenderit in voluptate nonumy. Minimum veniami quis nostrud laboris nisi ut aliquip ex ea com dolor in reprehenderit in voluptate nonumy.

Lorum ipsum dolor sit amet, con; minimim venami quis nostrud laboris nisi ut aliquip ex ea com dolor in reprehenderit in voluptate nonumy. Minimum veniami quis nostrud laboris nisi ut aliquip ex ea com dolor in reprehenderit in

continued on page 15

continued from page 1

reprehenderit in voluptate nonumy. Minimum veniami quis nostrud laboris nisi ut aliquip ex ea com dolor in reprehenderit in voluptate nonumy.

Lorum ipsum dolor sit amet, con; minimim venami quis nostrud laboris nisi ut aliquip ex ea com dolor in reprehenderit in voluptate nonumy.

Lorum ipsum dolor sit amet, con; minimim venami quis nostrud laboris nisi ut aliquip ex ea com dolor in reprehenderit in voluptate nonumy. Minimum veniami quis

Moving On

By now you have some understanding of the basic elements of graphic design. In the next two chapters, you'll learn how to manipulate those elements to enhance the communicating power of your printed materials.

Chapter 3: Building Blocks of Design

The basic tools used to create graphic design never change.

Although the technology has changed considerably, the basic tools used to create effective graphic design never change. The very tools used by the earliest cavemen are also relevant today with the latest desktop publishing hardware and software. In this chapter, you'll learn some of those fundamental tools, which will become second nature as you develop your desktop publishing skills.

White Space

Use white space–or blank space, free of text or artwork–to add contrast to your publications.

One of the most important building blocks of effective graphic design, white space provides contrast. It also provides a resting point for the reader's eyes, as they begin moving through the publication. White space can take many forms.

A. White space can be the open area surrounding a headline. The readability of a headline often is enhanced more by adding white space around it than by increasing type size.

B. The margins of an advertisement or publication are white space. Wide margins push the reader's attention into the center of the page.

C. The space between columns of type is white space. The wider the columns, the more space there should be between them.

White space can be used creatively to open up a page.

D. The space at the ends of lines of unjustified or ragged-right type is white space.

E. Indented sentences have white space.

F. White space also refers to the area between lines of type. Tightly packed lines of type "darken" a publication.

G. White space also can be added between paragraphs to "open up" a publication.

It's important to note that white space doesn't have to be "white." If your publication is printed on colored paper stock (e.g., ivory or tan), white space permits more of the background color to appear.

A.

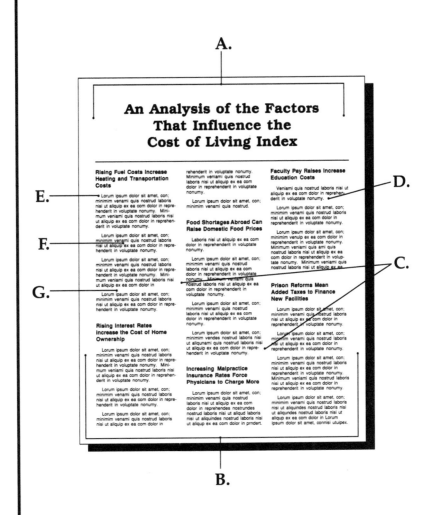

An Analysis of the Factors
That Influence the
Cost of Living Index

Rising Fuel Costs Increase Heating and Transportation Costs

Lorum ipsum dolor sit amet, con; minimim venami quis nostrud laboris nisi ut aliquip ex ea com dolor in reprehenderit in voluptate nonumy. Minimum veniami quis nostrud laboris nisi ut aliquip ex ea com dolor in reprehenderit in voluptate nonumy.

Lorum ipsum dolor sit amet, con; minimim venami quis nostrud laboris nisi ut aliquip ex ea com dolor in reprehenderit in voluptate nonumy.

Lorum ipsum dolor sit amet, con; minimim venami quis nostrud laboris nisi ut aliquip ex ea com dolor in reprehenderit in voluptate nonumy. Minimum veniami quis nostrud laboris nisi ut aliquip ex ea com dolor in

Lorum ipsum dolor sit amet, con; minimim venami quis nostrud laboris nisi ut aliquip ex ea com dolor in reprehenderit in voluptate nonumy.

Rising Interest Rates Increase the Cost of Home Ownership

Lorum ipsum dolor sit amet, con; minimim venami quis nostrud laboris nisi ut aliquip ex ea com dolor in reprehenderit in voluptate nonumy. Minimum veniami quis nostrud laboris nisi ut aliquip ex ea com dolor in reprehenderit in voluptate nonumy.

Lorum ipsum dolor sit amet, con; minimim venami quis nostrud laboris nisi ut aliquip ex ea com dolor in reprehenderit in voluptate nonumy.

Lorum ipsum dolor sit amet, con; minimim venami quis nostrud laboris nisi ut aliquip ex ea com dolor in

rehenderit in voluptate nonumy. Minimum veniami quis nostrud laboris nisi ut aliquip ex ea com dolor in reprehenderit in voluptate nonumy.

Lorum ipsum dolor sit amet, con; minimim venami quis nostrud.

Food Shortages Abroad Can Raise Domestic Food Prices

Laboris nisi ut aliquip ex ea com dolor in reprehenderit in voluptate nonumy.

Lorum ipsum dolor sit amet, con; minimim venami quis nostrud laboris nisi ut aliquip ex ea com dolor in reprehenderit in voluptate nonumy. Minimum veniami quis nostrud laboris nisi ut aliquip ex ea com dolor in reprehenderit in voluptate nonumy.

Lorum ipsum dolor sit amet, con; minimim venami quis nostrud laboris nisi ut aliquip ex ea com dolor in reprehenderit in voluptate nonumy.

Lorum ipsum dolor sit amet, con; minimim vendes nostrud laboris nisi ut aliqunami quis nostrud laboris nisi ut aliquip ex ea com dolor in reprehenderit in voluptate nonumy.

Increasing Malpractice Insurance Rates Force Physicians to Charge More

Lorum ipsum dolor sit amet, con; minimim venami quis nostrud laboris nisi ut aliquip ex ea com dolor in reprehendes nostrundes nostrud laboris nisi ut aliqud laboris nisi ut aliquindes nostrud laboris nisi ut aliquip ex ea com dolor in prndert.

Faculty Pay Raises Increase Education Costs

Veniami quis nostrud laboris nisi ut aliquip ex ea com dolor in reprehenderit in voluptate nonumy.

Lorum ipsum dolor sit amet, con; minimim venami quis nostrud laboris nisi ut aliquip ex ea com dolor in reprehenderit in voluptate nonumy.

Lorum ipsum dolor sit amet, con; minimim venulp ex ea com dolor in reprehenderit in voluptate nonumy. Minimum veniami quis ami quis nostrud laboris nisi ut aliquip ex ea com dolor in reprehenderit in voluptate nonumy. Minimum veniami quis nostrud laboris nisi ut aliquip ex ea

Prison Reforms Mean Added Taxes to Finance New Facilities

Lorum ipsum dolor sit amet, con; minimim venami quis nostrud laboris nisi ut aliquip ex ea com dolor in reprehenderit in voluptate nonumy.

Lorum ipsum dolor sit amet, con; minimim venami quis nostrud laboris nisi ut aliquip ex ea com dolor in reprehenderit in voluptate nonumy.

Lorum ipsum dolor sit amet, con; minimim venami quis nostrud laboris nisi ut aliquip ex ea com dolor in reprehenderit in voluptate nonumy. Minimum veniami quis nostrud laboris nisi ut aliquip ex ea com dolor in reprehenderit in voluptate nonumy.

Lorum ipsum dolor sit amet, con; minimim venami quis nostrud laboris nisi ut aliquindes nostrud laboris nisi ut aliquip ex ea com dolor in Lorum ipsum dolor sit amet, connisi utuipex.

E.

F.

G.

D.

C.

B.

The type you choose and the way it's placed on a page can help your reader understand your message.

The Language of Type

Type–the size, shape and spacing of the letters that make up words– influences the appearance of your advertisement, book, brochure or newsletter more than any other single visual element.

The type you choose and the way it's placed on a page can help, or hinder, your reader's ability to understand your message.

Type is specified by face, style, size, alignment and spacing.

Typeface

Choose a typeface that "speaks" to your readers in the tone of voice most appropriate to your publication.

Typeface refers to the style–or shape–of the letters and numbers.

Hundreds of typefaces are available, each representing its designer's unique approach to clarity and expressiveness. Each typeface influences the tone of the publication by changing the way readers "say" each word to themselves. Typefaces can be

Formal

NEWSY

TECHNICAL

Contemporary

Ornate

Although hundreds of typefaces are available, they fall into two major categories: serif and sans-serif.

Serif Type

Use serif typefaces for body copy.

Serif type is categorized by tiny decorations or "feet" attached to the edges of each letter. Those "feet" serve both decorative and functional purposes. They not only add visual "character" to the letters, they also help guide the reader's eye movement from letter to letter. This helps the reader see your message in terms of words and sentences instead of as individual letters.

Serif type usually is formed by vertical and horizontal strokes of different thicknesses.

B

One of the most frequently used serif typefaces, Times Roman is built into most laser printers or is available from most type vendors.

Other frequently used serif typefaces include

New Century Schoolbook

Souvenir

Bookman

Palatino

Because the "feet" provide letter-to-letter transitions, serif typefaces are ideal for body copy.

Sans-serif Type

Use sans-serif type for headlines. Sans-serif type is, literally, what the name implies: type that lacks the decorative flourishes of serif type.

In addition, the characters of sans-serif typefaces usually have the same thickness at all points, unlike serif typefaces which vary in thickness.

When used in small doses, sans-serif type has a boldness and simplicity that add impact.

When used in small doses, sans-serif type has a boldness and simplicity that add impact. But large amounts of sans-serif type are difficult to read.

Sans-serif typefaces are best used in large sizes, particularly when surrounded by plenty of white space, such as in headlines.

FIRE SALE!

Upper case headlines are best used when the message is short and to the point. Upper case headlines are best used when the message is short and to the point. Upper case headlines are best used when the message is short and to the point. Upper case headlines are best used when the message is short and to the point.

Upper case headlines are best used when the message is short and to the point. Upper case headlines are best used when the message is short and to the point. Upper case headlines are best used when the message is short and to the point.

Upper case headlines are best used when the message is short and to the point. Upper case headlines are best used when the message is short and to the point. Upper case headlines are best used when the message is

short and to the point. Upper case headlines are best used when the message is short and to the point. Upper case headlines are best used when the message is short and to the point. Upper case headlines are best used when the message is short and to the point.

Upper case headlines are best used when the message is short and to the point. Upper case headlines are best used when the message is short and to the point. Upper case headlines are best used when the message is short and to the point.

Upper case headlines are best used when the message is short and to the point. Upper case headlines are best used

Helvetica, the best-known sans-serif typeface, is built into most laser printers.

Other popular sans-serif typefaces include

Optima

Avant Garde

Type Style

Type style refers to the way each typeface can be modified to add contrast or emphasis.

On most desktop publishing systems, the style options that come with the laser printer include

normal, **bold,** *italics and **bold italics.***

Use bold type for authority or emphasis, or to "darken" a page. Bold type is frequently used for subheads, which break up long expanses of body copy.

Use bold type for authority or emphasis.

Use italics for added emphasis, often with overtones of irony or humor. In addition, italics often are used for captions.

Use italics for added emphasis.

Not only was he late, he was *very* late.

Use bold italics to make a point really stand out.

Type Weight

Weight gives you further flexibility in using type to influence the appearance and "tone" of your publication.

Additional type variations are available as downloadable fonts, which can be added to your desktop publishing system and called upon as needed.

For example, in the Helvetica family, Helvetica Condensed Black has heavier impact than Helvetica Condensed Bold. Helvetica Condensed Black is an ideal choice for big, bold headlines.

BOLD WINS

Helvetica Light gives headlines a delicate appearance and "lightens" a page.

The Prima Ballerina

Helvetica Narrow is yet another typeface option. The width of the characters has been mathematically compressed, allowing more letters to be included on each line. Helvetica Narrow often is used for subheads and business forms.

This Is Helvetica Narrow

Type Size

Type size should be proportionate to both the importance of the message and its surroundings.

Type can be as large or small as you desire.

Type is measured in points. There are 72 points to the inch. Most desktop publishing systems allow you to adjust type size in half-point increments.

Type size should be appropriate to the typeface, as well as line length and line spacing.

But, once again, type size cannot be considered alone. Type size should be appropriate to the typeface, as well as line length and line spacing.

Small type adrift in a sea of white space appears "lost."

Where am I?

Large type squeezed into a small area is hard to read and is visually disturbing and claustrophobic.

Over Here, Taking Up All Available Space!

Be aware that different typefaces vary in length. For example, two different typefaces, each set in 18-point type, result in different line lengths.

One, Two, Three, Four, Five
One, Two, Three, Four, Five

Spacing

Adjust leading—or the vertical spacing between lines of type—to improve the appearance and readability of your advertisement or publication.

Leading describes the amount of space separating a line of type from the line above it and the line below it. Leading is as important as type size.

The default, or "automatic" line spacing, found on most desktop publishing systems adds approximately 20 percent to the basic type size. Thus, the default for 10-point type is 12-point leading.

Headlines improve in appearance and readability when leading is reduced. Ideally, leading should make your headline appear as a unit. Because readers grasp headlines as a series of words, the words should stand together as an entity.

default   adjusted

Extra leading often improves the appearance of body copy. It "opens up" the page and makes it less "gray."

Extra leading opens up the page and makes it less gray.

default   adjusted

You, of course, want to avoid leading so spacious that readers get lost when their eyes leave the end of one line and try to find the beginning of the next line.

Leading should be in proportion to line length. In general, use narrow leading for short lines of type. Increase leading as line length increases.

By tightening the tracking, you increase the density of your body copy, fitting more words into the same amount of space.

Leading also can be used as a design tool. Sometimes you might want to tighten leading so that descenders from one line of headline type touch the ascenders from the line below.

Symbolic
Connections, Inc.

That lets you create special effects, particularly in designing logos and mastheads.

Tracking and Kerning

You can improve the appearance and readability of your headlines by adjusting the spacing between letters.

Tracking allows you to adjust letter spacing throughout an advertisement or publication.

> **In the course of human events, it may become necessary to adjust tracking to subtly fit more words on a page.**

By tightening the tracking, you increase the density of your body copy, fitting more words into the same amount of space. That "darkens" a publication.

> **In the course of human events, it may become necessary to adjust tracking to subtly fit more words on a page.**

Kerning enhances the reader's ability to look at a headline as a sentence rather than as a series of individual letters.

Certain pairs of letters, if set normally, appear to be separated by too much space. That's particularly apparent in headlines containing upper-case T's next to lower-case o's, upper-case Y's next to lower-case a's, etc.

Yo-Yo   WAVE
Yo-Yo   WAVE

Kerning reduces the spaces between individual pairs of letters. It enhances the reader's ability to look at a headline as a sentence, or group of words, rather than as a series of individual letters.

Kerning can be expanded for special effects, such as spacing a word across the top of a column or publication. Expanded letter spacing converts a word into a graphic element or piece of art.

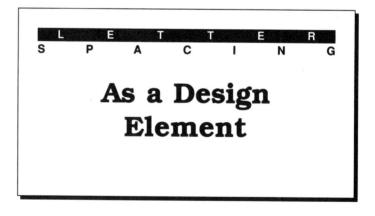

Word Spacing

Adjust word spacing to increase or decrease the density of type.

When words are closer together, more words can be included on each line. In certain situations, that also can reduce the number of hyphenated–or split–words.

Word spacing should be adjusted with care. If you reduce word spacing too much, the text becomes difficult to read and the publication becomes "dark."

Paragraph Spacing

Add extra space between paragraphs to enhance readability.

Extra space between paragraphs makes each paragraph appear more like a self-contained unit. It also adds "air" to the publication by breaking up the "grayness" of large expanses of copy.

Extra space between paragraphs makes each appear more like a self-contained unit.

> **Prison Reforms Mean Added Taxes to Finance New Facilities**
>
> Lorum ipsum dolor sit amet, con; minimim venami quis nostrud laboris nisi ut aliquip ex ea com dolor in reprehenderit in voluptate nonumy.
>
> Lorum ipsum dolor sit amet, con; minimim venami quis nostrud laboris nisi ut aliquipiquip ex ea com dolor in reprehenderit in voluptate nonumy. Minimum veniami ex ea com dolor in reprehenderit in voluptate nonumy.
>
> Lorum ipsum dolor sit amet, con; minimim venami quis nostrud laboris nisi ut aliquip ex ea com dolor in reprehenderit in voluptate nonumy. Minimum veniami quis nostrud laboris nisi ut aliquip ex ea com dolor in reprehenderit in voluptate nonumy.
>
> Lorum ipsum dolor sit amet, con; minimim venami quis nostrud

Tabs and Indents

Use tabs and indents to emphasize paragraph divisions and set off extended quotations.

Tabs can be used in conjunction with extra space between paragraphs to further "open up" a publication.

Tabs can be used to further "open up" a publication.

> **Prison Reforms Mean Added Taxes to Finance New Facilities**
>
> Lorum ipsum dolor sit amet, con; minimim venami quis nostrud laboris nisi ut aliquip ex ea com dolor in reprehenderit in voluptate nonumy.
>
> Lorum ipsum dolor sit amet, con; minimim venami quis nostrud laboris nisi ut aliquipiquip ex ea com dolor in reprehenderit in voluptate nonumy. Minimum veniami ex ea com dolor in reprehenderit in voluptate nonumy.
>
> Lorum ipsum dolor sit amet, con; minimim venami quis nostrud laboris nisi ut aliquip ex ea com dolor in reprehenderit in voluptate nonumy. Minimum veniami quis nostrud laboris nisi ut aliquip ex ea com dolor in reprehenderit in voluptate nonumy.
>
> Lorum ipsum dolor sit amet, con; minimim venami quis nostrud

In addition to calling attention to quotations, indents can be used to give equal importance to a series of items organized in a list.

Bills to Pay
1. IRS
2. Home Mortgage
3. Car Payment
4. Utilities
5. Medical Insurance
6. Hobby Shop

Alignment

Choose type alignment most appropriate for its purpose. Type can be placed in a column in several ways.

Type is normally organized flush left, meaning the first letters of each line of type are aligned.

However, the ends of lines (right-hand side) can be set in a justified or ragged-right column. The option you choose influences the "color" and tone of your publication, as well as the cost.

Flush-left/ragged-right type creates informal, contemporary, "open" advertisements and publications. Each word is separated by the same amount of space. Few words are hyphenated–or split by syllable between two lines. Flush-left/ragged-right lines generally end where words end. Only the longest words are hyphenated. The irregular line endings create white space, which lightens a publication. In addition, because few words are hyphenated, readers instantly recognize groups of letters as words, instead of being forced to mentally assemble words from letters appearing at the right-hand edge of one line and the left-hand edge of the next.

Flush-left/ragged-right type creates informal, contemporary, "open" ads and publications.

Lorum ipsum dolor saedit
amet, coeten minimim
venami quis nostrud
laboris nisi ut aliqui dolor in
reprehenderit in voluptate
nonumy. Minimum
veniami quis nostrud

Justified, or flush-left/flush-right type, is characterized by lines of equal length. The first letters and last letters of each line are aligned. Equal line length is achieved by adjusting the tracking (spacing between words).

Because white space is missing, justified columns "darken" a publication. In addition, justified type is considered more difficult to read, because it contains more hyphenated words.

Many magazines and newspapers use justified type because the word density is higher. As a result, fewer pages and less space are needed to communicate the same amount of information.

Lorum ipsum dolor saedit ameit, coeten minimim venami quis nostrud laboris nisi ut aliqui doelor in reprehenderit opn voluptate nonumy. Minimum eix veniami quis nostrud laboris nisi ut

Many magazines and newspapers use justified type because the word density is higher.

Type also can be centered, which is particularly useful for short headlines that span more than one column of type.

Avoid long centered blocks of type, such as headlines spread over three or four lines. Those are more difficult to read, because readers have to search for the beginning of each line.

Offshore Production Cost Increases for Consumer Electronics and Cars Tied to Rising Standards of Living

Lorum ipsum dolor sit amet, con minimim venami quis nostrud laboris nisi ut aliquip ex ea com dolor in repre- henderit in voluptate nonumy. Minimum veniami quis nostrud laboris nisi ut aliquip ex ea com dolor in reprehenderit in voluptate nonumy.
Lorum ipsum dolor sit amet, con;

Type also can be set flush right, ragged left.

Because readers normally read from left to right, flush-right type should be used with discretion. Flush-right type forces the reader to slow down and spend time creating and identifying words out of individual letters.

Because people read from left to right, flush-right type should be used with discretion.

Reading flush-right copy takes more time because your eyes have to search for the beginning of each line.

Runarounds

Use runarounds, or lines of irregular length, to fill the white space created around irregularly shaped photographs or illustrations.

Runarounds are an effective way to eliminate excess white space around irregularly shaped artwork. Runarounds also can tie artwork and body copy together cohesively.

Runarounds tie artwork and copy together.

Distortion

Stretch or compress type to create special effects, such as on mast-heads and logos.

Most desktop publishing programs allow you to stretch or compress individual letters or even words and sentences. Stretching and compressing type blur the distinction between "type" and "artwork," converting words into graphic elements.

Stretching and compressing type convert words into graphic elements.

STRETCH

COMPRESS

Moving On

That completes our survey of the basic elements of graphic design. However, there will be times when you'll want to draw attention to key ideas or supporting concepts. Those concepts may either be text or graphic. In the next chapter, you'll learn how to improve your publication by selectively adding emphasis to your most important thoughts.

Chapter 4: Tools of Emphasis

The tools of empha-
sis are most effec-
tive when used
with restraint.

The tools of emphasis add color and contrast to your advertisement or publication and enhance its communicating power by directing interest to important points. These tools must be used with restraint; otherwise, the exceptional becomes the norm, making it difficult to separate the important from the unimportant.

Reverses

Emphasize headlines or short sentences by using white type against a black background.

Reversed type is particularly effective for short sentences set in large, sans-serif upper- and lower-case type.

Reverses lose impact if they're hard to read, which often occurs when type is too small.

> Notice how the words run together and are difficult to read when reversed type is set too small

Reverses lose impact when type is too small.

Use reversed serif typefaces with discretion. The letters tend to lose definition.

Screens

Emphasize headlines and important passages by placing them against a gray background.

Screens can add contrast and enhance the readability of your publication in many ways.

For example, use white type against a dark gray background.

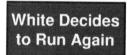

> **White Decides to Run Again**

Screens add emphasis to your copy.

Or, use black type against a light gray background.

> **Reduced Contrast Is Sometimes a Virtue**

Screens are particularly effective when used in conjunction with rules or boxes. They're an important technique for calling attention to sidebars—small, self-contained articles that provide additional information about a topic mentioned in a larger feature story.

Color

You can use color in several ways to add impact to your advertisement or publication without going to the expense of four-color printing.

1) Use a non-standard paper color. Hundreds of paper colors are available at a slightly higher cost than standard.

When planning your print schedule, take into account the fact that some color papers may need to be specially ordered—but the effect is usually worth it. Be sure that the paper color you've chosen provides sufficient contrast to make the ink you've chosen stand out. Creams and tans are always safe choices. Bright colored papers should be used with discretion.

2) Use a custom ink color. Other than inertia, there's no reason to feel you always have to use standard, out-of-the-can colors for your publication. Excellent effects can be achieved by using custom ink colors, particularly the darker shades of gray.

Ink colors are referred to by their PMS number. PMS stands for Pantone Matching System, a universal method of specifying exact ink shades. PMS colors cost a bit more than standard, out-of-the-bucket inks—referred to as "process" colors—but the effect is worth it. PMS colors are custom-mixed. When you specify "PMS 431," a printer in Portland, Oregon, and a printer in Portland, Maine, both will know the exact shade you want.

3) Add a second color to your publication. Use the second color for selected parts of your publication—borders, rules, subheads, masthead or logo. Avoid over-use of a second ink color. Remember: less is more.

Choose a second color that creates a pleasing contrast to the primary ink color. Avoid choosing colors that are similar to the primary color.

PMS colors cost a bit more than standard inks, but the effect is worth it.

Avoid over-using a second ink color.

Color used on certain parts of a page is called spot color.

4) Use blocks of color to provide a background for an entire page with reversed headlines or blocks of copy.

Bleeds

Blocks of color—or large photographs—that extend to the edges of a page are called bleeds.

Bleeds work particularly well with brochures, in which the entire front and rear covers are printed in a second color, with headlines reversed out.

With bleeds, reversed headlines appear in the color of the paper, creating a three-color effect.

Kickers

Tease readers into reading your headline with a kicker, a short phrase that summarizes the headline.

Kickers can introduce the headline by relating it to other articles or existing information. Kickers also can categorize a headline.

Use kickers to arouse reader's curiosity.

Drop Caps

Use over-sized first letters to emphasize the first sentence of an article or to introduce a new section of an article.

When used in an advertisement, over-sized capital letters provide an important visual transition between the headline and body copy.

C ipsum dolor sit amet, con; minimim venami quis nostrud laboris nisi ut aliquip ex ea com dolor in reprehenderit in voluptate nonumy. Minimum veniami quis nostrud laboris nisi ut aliquip ex ea com dolor in reprehenderit in voluptate nonumy.

Lorum ipsum dolor sit amet, con; minimim venami quis nostrud laboris nisi ut aliquip ex ea com dolor in reprehenderit in voluptate nonumy.

Lorum ipsum dolor sit amet, con; minimim venami quis nostrud laboris nisi ut aliquip ex ea com dolor in reprehenderit in voluptate nonumy.

Drop caps add visual interest.

Sinks

Use extra white space at the top of each page to emphasize body copy.

Extra white space at the top of a page forces attention to the body copy.

That extra white space forces attention to the body copy below it.

Handling Artwork

Use photographs, illustrations, graphs and charts to increase the communicating power of your publications.

Your choice of artwork has as much of an impact on the appearance and communicating power of your publication as your choice of type. Artwork can be modified in numerous ways.

Photographs

Use photographs to communicate as literally as possible.

Photographs tell a story in a straightforward way. Their effectiveness is determined by their inherent quality, as well as their placement on the page.

Cropping

Eliminate unimportant details by cropping.

Cropping involves removing unwanted photo details by cutting in from the top, bottom or sides of the photo.

Photographs tell a story in a straight-forward way.

In most cases, the photograph retains a rectangular or square shape.

Silhouetting

Emphasize important details by silhouetting.

Silhouetting, or masking, eliminates unimportant background details and changes the photograph's shape.

**Silhouetting elimi-
nates unimportant
background details.**

The shape of the resulting photograph is determined by the shape of the details you want to emphasize.

Boxes

Place important photographs inside boxes.

The borders of those boxes can be as thick or as thin as you like.

Boxes can square off silhouetted photographs, allowing important details to emerge without breaking an established format.

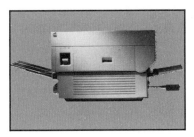

Drop Shadows and Size

Use drop shadows to draw attention to photographs.

Place photographs and illustrations in boxes with drop shadows to create an attention-getting, three-dimensional effect.

When several photographs are used together, make the most important photograph dramatically larger than the others.

Use smaller photographs to provide contrast and support the message of the primary photograph.

Drop shadows draw attention to photographs.

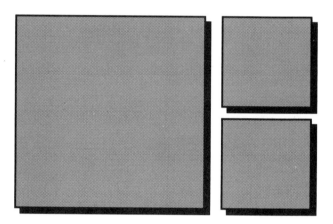

When no single photograph is more important than the others, arrange them in a repeating sequence.

Bleeds

Extend important photographs to the top or side edges of your advertisement or publication.

Photos can extend to page edges.

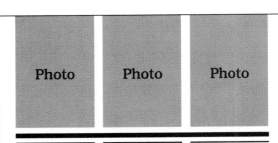

That technique draws attention to the photographs by allowing them to overwhelm adjacent margins and borders.

Illustrations

Illustrations also can be manipulated to increase their communicating power and improve the appearance of your publication.

Like photographs, illustrations can be cropped, boxed, silhouetted, placed against screened or reversed backgrounds, or allowed to bleed to the edge of your advertisement or publication.

Illustrations created with draw-type programs also can be distorted. For example, you can stretch the illustration vertically to make it taller.

Illustrations can be manipulated to increase communicating power.

Or, you can stretch the illustration horizontally to make it wider.

Illustrations created with draw-type programs also can be compressed horizontally or vertically.

Most important, illustrations created with paint-type programs can be manipulated to create very dramatic effects.

As paint-type or scanned illustrations are increased in size, the dot pattern of which they're composed becomes more and more obvious. This can be used to create attention-getting "impressionistic" effects that often have more communicating power than the original illustration.

Dot patterns can be used to create attention-getting effects.

The basis for an impressionistic drawing might be a scanned photograph.

Moving On

In the previous two chapters, you've learned how using the tools of organization and emphasis can enhance your documents' communicating power. The next chapter covers common misapplication of these tools, which can hinder your publications' message and design.

Chapter 5: Ten Common Design Pitfalls

The power and flexibility built into desktop publishing software make it easy to create overly complicated documents that hinder readership.

The following illustrations show some of the more commonly encountered examples of "desktop publishing overkill." These samples show how the desire to make full use of various desktop publishing capabilities can work against the goals of the straightforward writer-to-reader communication.

Irregularly Shaped Blocks of Copy

Avoid the temptation to show off your desktop publishing program's ability to set type in irregular shapes.

Desktop publishing programs may tempt you to ignore the precept that readers read–or decode–words from left to right. Desktop publishing programs make it too easy to create complicated runarounds and irregularly shaped blocks of type.

Flush-left type is easiest to read.

It might be fun to set body copy in the shape of a diamond, Christmas tree or reindeer, but chances are those special effects diminish the overall effectiveness of your communication.

Flush-left type is easiest to read. Blocks of type with irregular line beginnings take more time to read and can cause readers to lose track of the beginning of the next line they're trying to find.

Angled Type

Avoid the temptation to set type at an angle.

Columns of flush-left type are easy to read. Angled type requires more effort.

Lorum ipsum dolor sit amet,
venami quis nostrud laboris
aliquip ex ea com dolor in rep
derit in voluptate nonumy. Min
veniami quis nostrud laboris nisi

Type that goes uphill or downhill may attract attention, but slows reading. Readers are forced to tilt their heads or tilt the publication...or move on without reading the type.

Angled type is only permissible in short banners, or "teasers," placed on the upper front corners of magazines or newsletters.

Angled type is permissible in short banners, or "teasers."

Excess Underlining

Use discretion when underlining.

Use bold-faced or italicized type instead of underlining.

Avoid excess underlining.

<u>When more than a few words are underlined, the readers' eyes become confused. Readers have difficulty separating the words from the horizontal lines because their eyes fluctuate between the underlining and the words.</u>

In addition, descenders often become lost in the underlining, making the letters harder to identify.

Widows and Orphans

Avoid widows and orphans.

A widow is a word or syllable isolated at the bottom of a column or paragraph.

Widows can usually be eliminated by editing the text.

> Con minimim venami quis nostrud laboris nisi ut aliquip ex ea com dolor in in nostrud ami quis nostrud laboris nisi ut aliquip ex ea com do minimim venami quis nostrud laboris iquip ex ea com dolor in in nostrud ami quis nostrud laboris nisi ut aliquip.

Orphans are words isolated at the top of a column.

> lorum ip.
>
> Con minimim venami quis nostrud laboris nisi ut aliquip ex ea com dolor in in nostrud ami quis nostrud laboris nisi ut aliquip ex ea com do minimim venami quis nostrud laboris nisi ut aliquip ex ea com

Widows and orphans can usually be eliminated by editing the text. Often, adding or subtracting a word or two from a paragraph is enough to adjust line endings, thereby eliminating those unsightly transgressions.

Unequal Spacing

Strive for consistent spacing between the elements that make up an advertisement or publication.

The human eye is extremely sensitive to tiny variations in spacing. Unequal spacing is immediately perceived as "sloppy" and "unworthy of serious notice."

Pay particular attention to

- Spacing between headlines and the top and side borders.

- Headlines and body copy

The human eye is extremely sensitive to variations in spacing.

- Subheads and body copy

- Captions and artwork
- Artwork and body copy

Lorum ipsum dolor sit amet, con; minimim venami quis nostrud laboris nisi ut aliquip ex ea com dolor in reprehenderit in voluptate nonumy.

Inconsistent spacing indicates a careless attitude, telling readers that your message isn't important.

- Column endings and bottom margins

Readers subconsciously place a great deal of emphasis on those tiny details. Inconsistent spacing indicates a careless attitude, which indicates that your message isn't very important.

Exaggerated Tabs and Indents

When placing text from word processed files, tabs and indents should be adjusted to compensate for type size and column width.

Often, when type is placed without modification, the first lines of each paragraph are indented too deeply. Proper tab spacing should be based on type size, as well as column width. Wide columns and large type sizes usually have deep tabs and indents. Narrow columns and small type sizes shouldn't be indented as deeply.

Adjust tabs proportional to column widths.

Prison Reforms Mean Added Taxes to Finance New Facilities

Lorum ipsum dolor sit amet, con; minimim venami quis nostrud laboris nisi ut aliquip ex ea com dolor in reprehenderit in voluptate nonumy.

Lorum ipsum dolor sit amet, con; minimim venami quis nostrud laboris nisi ut aliquip ex ea com dolor in reprehenderit in voluptate nonumy.

Prison Reforms Mean Added Taxes to Finance New Facilities

Lorum ipsum dolor sit amet, con; minimim venami quis nostrud laboris nisi ut aliquip ex ea com dolor in reprehenderit in voluptate nonumy.

Lorum ipsum dolor sit amet, con; minimim venami quis nostrud laboris nisi ut aliquip ex ea com dolor in reprehenderit in voluptate nonumy.

Excessive Hyphenation

Switch to manual hyphenation or adjust the hyphenation zone when too many words are hyphenated.

Reduce hyphenation to a minimum.

<table>
<tr>
<td>

Prison Reforms Mean Added Taxes to Finance New Facilities

Lorum ipsum dolor-sit amet, con; mini-mimvenami quisnos-trud laboris nisi ut aliq-uip ex ea com dolor in reprehenderit involup-tate nonumy.

Lorum ipsum dolor-sit amet, con; mini-mimvenami quisnos-trud laboris nisi ut aliq-uip ex ea com dolor in reprehenderit involup-tate nonumy.

Lorum ipsum dolor-sit amet, con; mini-mimve nami quisnos-trud laboris nisi ut aliq-uip ex ea com dolor in

</td>
<td>

Prison Reforms Mean Added Taxes to Finance New Facilities

Lorum ipsum dolor-sit amet, con; minimimvenami quisnostrud laboris nisi ut aliquip ex ea com dolor in reprehenderit involuptate nonumy.

Lorum ipsum dolor-sit amet, con; minimimvenami quisnostrud laboris nisi ut aliquip ex ea com dolor in reprehenderit involuptate nonumy.

Lorum ipsum dolor-sit amet, con; minimimve nami quisnostrud laboris nisi ut aliquip ex eiquip ex ea com doa com dolor in reprehenderit involuptate nonumy.

Lorum ipsum dolor sit amet, con; minimim venami quis nostrud laboris nisi ut aliquip ex ea com dolor in reprehenderit iiquip ex ea com don voluptate nonumy. Minimum veniami quis nostrud laboris nisi ut aliquip ex ea com dolor in reprehiquip ex ea com doenderit in voluptate nonumy.

</td>
</tr>
</table>

Excessive hyphenation often occurs in narrow columns of type.

That can be corrected by reducing type size, increasing column width or choosing flush-left/ragged-right alignment. It can also be corrected by increasing the hyphenation zone, which permits longer words at the end of each line, although excessive word spacing might result.

Another alternative involves switching to manual hyphenation. That gives you control over which words are hyphenated and which are moved intact to the next line.

Grammatical Errors

Carefully proofread your publication before you print a final copy.

In particular, avoid placing too much trust in spell-check programs. They differ from program to program in the types of errors they can detect.

Some programs, for example, can't identify repeated words.

Financial trouble trouble ahead.

Other programs can't identify words with improper capitalization or numbers (or punctuation) mixed in with letters.

New york wins world Series

Avoid placing too much trust in spell-check programs.

And no spell-check program can identify correctly spelled but improperly used words (e.g., "two" instead of "too," etc.).

Their goes Rodney

A two-step proofing process works best.

• First, read your completed manuscript aloud.

• Then have a second person read your work aloud.

It's easy to overlook your own errors, subconsciously supplying missing words or correcting misspelled words. Reading aloud makes it easy to catch these mistakes. Also, a second reader is less likely to subconsciously add missing words and is more likely to identify improperly used or misspelled words.

Cramped Logos and Addresses

Design your advertisements from the bottom up.

Often, a firm's logo, address, phone number and other buying information are difficult to read because they appear to be an afterthought. To avoid that, build your documents from the bottom up.

The logo and address in the top example look like they were added at the last minute. Addresses and phone numbers are difficult to read. In the bottom example, however, the logo and address are more readable.

Build your documents from the bottom up.

To eliminate that problem, you might create a separate graphic file consisting of your firm's logo, address and other information that will always appear in your materials. That file then can be easily added in a single step.

Too Many Typefaces

Avoid mixing typefaces, type sizes and weights on a single page.

The biggest single mistake most desktop publishers make is to include too many typefaces on a single page. This creates an amateurish, disorganized appearance.

Discipline yourself to practice restraint. Use the minimum number of typefaces, type sizes and weights necessary to organize your information and create a hierarchy of importance. Each change in typeface, size or weight slows down the reader.

Avoid the "ransom note" school of typography.

Moving On

Now that you're familiar with the basic philosophy of practical desktop design and the basic tools of organization and emphasis, it's time to apply that knowledge to specific advertisements, brochures, newsletters and other projects.

The examples in Section Two illustrate successful applications of the tools of graphic design. They also show how the appearance and communicating power of an advertisement or publication often can be greatly improved by simply rearranging the elements or providing greater contrast between them.

SECTION TWO

Putting Your Knowledge to Work

Chapter 6: Putting Your Knowledge to Work

Introduction

This section provides a gallery of graphic design examples that have been "made over," giving a before-and-after perspective.

The makeovers illustrate how basic graphic design elements can be used to improve the appearance and persuasiveness of your printed materials. You may be surprised to see how a common graphics problem can be resolved with a few minor changes.

Read this section in a "free-form" manner, focusing more on concepts rather than specific document types. For example, a three-column layout for an advertisement might work well for your newsletter. A more creative logo placement in a brochure also might provide a solution for your letterhead.

The examples and makeovers should help you understand how basic elements of graphic design work together to produce attractive printed materials.

Brochures (Original)

This flyer presents the reader with conflicting messages in the form of different typefaces, type styles and type sizes. Which message is most important? Which should be read first?

Contrasting type sizes and styles have been simplified to increase readability.

Contrasting margin treatments (sometimes centered, sometimes flush-left) have been reorganized to create easier eye movement.

NEW ENGLAND TURQUOISE
AND SILVER COMPANY

P.O. Box 2230 • 1 Bourbon Street • Peabody, MA 01960

To Place Orders ONLY: Call TOLL FREE **1-800-833-3328**
To Place Orders Inside Mass and for other Inquiries: Call (617) 535-5950

Early Fall Specials

Prices in effect from September 16, 1987 through October 31, 1987

All prices are approximate and subject to change without notice.
$50.00 MINIMUM ORDER
WHOLESALE ONLY   C.O.D. ONLY

Sterling Silver DIAMOND-CUT ITALIAN CROSSES
Back by Popular Demand, Quantities Limited – 6 for $6.50

18K Gold-Plated FINISHED CHAINS
All Lengths, All Styles $3.50 each or Assorted Lots of 12 or more $3.25 each

Choose from:

075 NUGGET 18", 20", 24"	100 HB NUGGET FLAT 18", 20", 24"
100 NUGGET 18", 20", 24"	120 HB NUGGET FLAT 18", 20", 24"
3mm ROPE 7", 8", 16", 18", 20", 24", 30"	065 HB LOVE 18", 20", 24"
4mm ROPE 7", 8", 16", 18", 20", 24", 30"	080 HB LOVE 18", 20", 24"
5mm ROPE 7", 8", 16", 18", 20", 24"	040 OVAL HB 18", 20", 24"
100 CURB 18", 20", 24"	060 HBB 18", 20", 24"
150 CURB 18", 20", 24"	080 HBB 18", 20", 24"
170 CURB 8", 18"	100 HBB 18", 20", 24"
170 OVAL CURB 7", 20", 24"	OPEN CURB 7", 8", 18", 20"
OVAL C-LINK 18", 20", 24"	HEAVY FIGAROA 7", 8", 18", 20"
100 HB FLORENTINE 18", 20", 24"	060 COBRA 18", 20", 24"

SILVERLUST on Sale through 10/31/87 ONLY!

Buy 12 Assorted Silverlust Bracelets (SLBR Series) – DEDUCT 10%
Buy 25 Assorted Silverlust Rings (SL Series – excluding SLR Mini Series) – DEDUCT 15%
Buy 12 Assorted Silverlust Slave Bracelets (SB Series) – DEDUCT 10%

Brochures (Makeover)

White space is essential in pieces which contain a lot of detailed information. Note how white space has been reorganized to direct readers' eyes to important body copy.

The "masthead" is maintained, but everything except the firm's logo and central message, "Early Fall Specials," is moved to the bottom, where readers are accustomed to finding such information.

A three-column grid is established, allowing readers easier access to product categories and item descriptions.

Each item is introduced by a subhead, set in the same typeface and size .

Addresses, phone numbers and ordering information are placed in a screened "Order Information" box at the bottom of the page.

The "call-to-action" telephone number is set in larger type.

New England Turquoise and Silver Company Presents

Early Fall Specials

Prices in effect from September 16, 1987 through October 31, 1987

18K Gold-Plated Finished Chains

All Lengths, All Styles $3.50 each of Assorted Lots of 12 or more $3.25 each. Choose from:

075 Nugget 18", 20", 24"
100 Nugget 18", 20", 24"

3mm Rope 7", 8", 16", 18", 20", 24", 30"
4mm Rope 7", 8", 16", 18", 20", 24", 30"
5mm Rope 7", 8", 16", 18", 20", 24"

100 Curb 18", 20", 24"
150 Curb 18", 20", 24"
170 Curb 18", 20"

170 Oval Curb 7", 20", 24"

Oval C-Link 18", 20", 24"

100 HB Florentine 18", 20", 24"

100 HB Nugget Flat 18", 20", 24"
120 HB Nugget Flat 18", 20", 24"

065 HB Love 18", 20.", 24"
080 HB Love 18", 20.", 24"

040 Oval HB 18", 20", 24"

060 HBB 18", 20", 24"
080 HBB 18", 20", 24"
100 HBB 18", 20", 24"

Open Curb 7", 8", 18", 20"

Heavy Figaroa 7", 8", 18", 20"

060 Cobra 18", 20", 24"

Silverlust on Sale through 10/31/87 only!

Buy 12 Assorted Silverlust Bracelets (SLBR Series) - Deduct 10%

Buy 25 Assorted Silverlust Rings (SL Series - excluding SLR Mini Series) - Deduct 15%

Buy 12 Assorted Silverlust Slave Bracelets (SB Series) - Deduct 10%

Sterling Silver Diamond-Cut Italian Crosses Back by Popular Demand, Quantities Limited - 6 for $6.50

NEW ENGLAND TURQUOISE
AND SILVER COMPANY

P. O. Box 2230
1 Bourbon Street
Peabody, MA 01960

Order Information

All prices are approximate and subject to change without notice. $50.00 Minimum order, wholesale only, C.O.D. only

To Place Orders ONLY: Call TOLL FREE 1-800-833-3328 Inside Mass. and for other inquiries call (617)535-5950

Advertisements (Original)

Ads and flyers built around conflicting illustrations and type styles make it difficult for the reader to quickly grasp the message.

Drawings of busy individuals answering telephones don't strengthen the image of a centralized, national answering service.

The space saved is devoted to a larger presentation of the headline's basic message—that Network Express makes it easy for customers to place an order.

By eliminating unnecessary duplication of telephone numbers, more emphasis can be placed on a single presentation.

Offer your customers the easiest possible way to place an order . . .

A 1-800 TOLL-FREE TELEPHONE NUMBER — NATIONWIDE!!

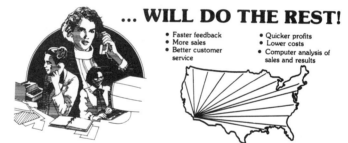

... WILL DO THE REST!

- Faster feedback
- More sales
- Better customer service

- Quicker profits
- Lower costs
- Computer analysis of sales and results

Network Express serves you — the direct response advertiser. We are committed to providing our clients with the best quality service in product marketing, lead generation and market research.

Our Operators are trained and ready to receive calls for: Catalog requests and orders; lead generation; dealer location; subscriptions; fund raising; etc.

We are qualified and experienced in all media sources: Television, Radio, Print advertising, Direct Mail, Catalogs, etc.

Call **1-800-541-0900** or **1-800-334-3030** in California and start using and benefitting from our TOLL-FREE service NOW!

NETWORK EXPRESS
993 SOUTH SANTA FE AVE., SUITE C
VISTA, CALIFORNIA 92083
1-800-541-0900
1-800-334-3030 in California

Advertisements (Makeover)

This piece is strengthened dramatically by restructuring it into a three-column format and reducing the number of visual elements.

The ad has been rebuilt around the only drawing with true communicating power— the map of the U.S.

The map has been stylized to reduce unnecessary detail.

A drop shadow effectively "pops" the map from the screened area.

The benefits of a nationwide 800 number prominently surround the illustration.

The bottom of the ad is weighted by Network Express's enlarged 800 numbers. Phone numbers and addresses should always appear prominently in advertising.

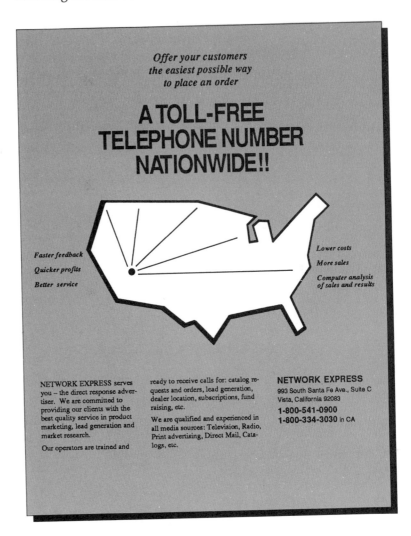

*Offer your customers
the easiest possible way
to place an order*

A TOLL-FREE
TELEPHONE NUMBER
NATIONWIDE!!

Faster feedback
Quicker profits
Better service

Lower costs
More sales
*Computer analysis
of sales and results*

NETWORK EXPRESS serves you – the direct response advertiser. We are committed to providing our clients with the best quality service in product marketing, lead generation and market research.

Our operators are trained and ready to receive calls for: catalog requests and orders, lead generation, dealer location, subscriptions, fund raising, etc.

We are qualified and experienced in all media sources: Television, Radio, Print advertising, Direct Mail, Catalogs, etc.

NETWORK EXPRESS
993 South Santa Fe Ave., Suite C
Vista, California 92083
1-800-541-0900
1-800-334-3030 in CA

Catalogs (Original)

Catalogs and price lists without illustrations present a unique set of design challenges. Type must be handled skillfully to avoid visual monotony.

Often, a highly symmetrical type treatment provides too little contrast to fully engage the reader.

Note how undifferentiated spacing creates a run-on effect, further discouraging readership.

NORMAN ROCKWELL
323 MAGAZINE COVERS
By Finch. 456 pages. Huge. 12 x 15¼. This magnificent, large-format, full color volume spans the artist's long and prolific career, reproducing 332 of his cover paintings for the SATURDAY EVENING POST, LADIES HOME JOURNAL and other magazines. Published at **$85.00**. Only **$45.00**.

GREAT MAGAZINE COVERS OF THE WORLD
By Kery. 384 pages. 9¼ x 12. A panorama of more than 500 great magazine covers (most reproduced in full color) from 20 countries, spanning a century-and-a-half of magazine publishing around the world. Including examples from 200 19th and 20th century magazines. Published at **$65.00**. Only **$45.00**.

VASARELY
150 pages. 9¾ x 13. 180 illustrations, including 64 full color plates. Masterful reproductions and a text by the artist combine to form an authoritative yet personal study of one of the major figures of modern art. Published at **$60.00**. Only **$35.00**.

CHAGALL BY CHAGALL
Sorlier. 262 pages. 11¼ x 12. 285 illustrations, including 83 full color plates. Illustrated autobiography. Published at **$50.00**. Only **$40.00**.

MAXFIELD PARRISH
By Ludwig. 223 pages. 9 x 12. 184 illustrations, 64 in full color. Published at **$25.00**. Only **$18.00**.

THE GREAT BOOK OF
FRENCH IMPRESSIONISM
By Kelder. 448 pages. 12 x 15¼. Over 400 illustrations, inlcuding 200 full color plates and 16 spectacular full color fold-outs. Huge, exquisitely produced treasury of French Impressionist art, packed with full-page reproductions. Examines the lives and works of all the major Impressionists and Post-Impressionists. Published at **$100.00**. Now **$59.95**.

CARL FABERGE
Goldsmith to the Imperial Court of Russia
By Snowman. 100 pages. 8¼ x 10½. Over 185 photos, 111 in full color. Originally Published at **$35.00**. Only **$22.00**.

CONTEMPORARY PAINTING
By Vogt. 135 pages. 7½ x 10½. Over 50 in full color. Penetrating analysis of post World War II European and American art. Including paintings by Jaspar Johns, Andy Warhol, Roy Lichtenstein, Jackson Pollock, others. **$19.95**. Now — **$14.95**.

TWENTIETH CENTURY MASTERS
OF EROTIC ART
By Smith. 212 pages. 9 x 12. 190 full color plates presents erotic works by such top-ranking artists as Picasso, Segal, Dali, Ernst, Rauschenberg, Rivers, Warhol, Schiele and others, many of which have never been displayed in public exhibitions. **$30.00**. Now — **$20.00**.

LEONARDO DA VINCI
538 pages. 11 x 14½. Huge. 1,635 illustrations, including many large full color plates. Originally published in Italy by the Instituto Geografico De Agostini, this new edition is the most lavish, authoritative ever produced. Published at **$60.00**. Only **$50.00**.

REMBRANDT PAINTINGS
By Gerson. 527 pages. 11 x 14½. Huge. Over 730 illustrations, including many large full color plates. Complete, authoritative and beautiful presentation of the great master's work. Written by one of the world's foremost Rembrandt authorities. The book was thirty years in the making in Amsterdam, and is lavishly illustrated with spectacular reproductions. Published at **$60.00**. Only **$50.00**.

ENGLISH CAMEO GLASS
By Grover. 480 pages. 8 x 11. A wealth of rare firsthand material and over 1,000 color and black and white plates makes this book an invaluable reference. Published at **$50.00**. Now **$25.00**.

20,000 YEARS OF WORLD PAINTING
By Jaffe. 416 pages. 9 x 13. Historical survey from early to modern art. 1,000 reproductions in full color. Was **$50.00** Now **$27.00**.

STAINED GLASS
By Seddon & Stephens. 205 pages. 473 full color photos. 11 x 14. Covers stained glass from the beginning to the present. Was **$39.95** Now **$19.95**.

THE COMPLETE BOOK OF EROTIC ART
By Kronhausen. 781 black and white plates. Extraordinary collection of the world's erotic art from Japan, China, India, Renaissance masters and modern greats. Originally Published in 2 Volumes at **$50.00**. New, Complete 1 Volume Editon Only **$25.00**.

COLLECTING POLITICAL AMERICANA
By Sullivan 1980. 250 pages. 8 x 11. 400 illustrations. Packed with reading. Out of print. **$15.95**. Now **$10.00**.

DIAMONDS
Myth, Magic and Reality Revised Edition. Over 420 full color illustrations. Beautiful and informative look at the world's most magnificent and mysterious stone. Tells how to recognize and appreciate quality stones, more. 288 pages. Large. 10¼ x 12. Originally Published at **$50.00**. Only **$29.95**.

THE GREAT BOOK OF JEWELS
By Heininger. 206 full color plates. 94 black and white photos. The most spectacular, lavishly illustrated, comprehensive volume ever published on jewels and jewelry. Nearly 300 photos specially made for this volume, many gems never available for public inspection before. Includes bibliography, table of gemstones; much more. Huge 11¾ x 13¾. Published at **$69.50**. Now **$29.95**.

10

Catalogs (Makeover)

Subtle changes in spacing and typefaces create contrast and promote readability.

The two-column format is retained, but body copy is set ragged right (instead of justified) to add contrast and break up type.

Titles now appear in sans-serif type, which provides more contrast to body copy.

The "Reference Art Books" logo (taken from the front cover) has been reversed and repeated on each page.

The firm's toll-free telephone numbers are repeated on each page, to create a strong, consistent response mechanism.

Norman Rockwell: 323 Magazine Covers
By Finch, 456 pages. Huge. 12 x 15 1/4. This magnificent, large-format, full color volume spans the artist's long and prolific career, reproduction 332 of his cover paintings for the SATURDAY EVENING POST, LADIES HOME JOURNAL and other magazines. Published at $85.00. Only **$45.00.**

Great Magazine Covers of the World
By Kery. 384 pages. 9 1/4 x 12. A panorama of more than 500 great magazine covers (most reproduced in full color) from 20 countries, spanning a century-and-a-half of magazine publishing around the world. Examples from 200 19th and 20th century magazines. Published at $65.00. Only **$45.00.**

Vasarely
150 page. 9 3/4 x 13. 180 illustrations, including 64 full color plates. Masterful reproductions and a text by the artist combine to form an authoritative yet personal study of one of the major figures of modern art. Published at $60.00. Only **$35.00.**

Chagall by Chagall
Sorlier. 262 pages. 11 1/4 x 12. 285 illustrations, including 83 full color plates. Illustrated autobiography. Published at $50.00. Only **$40.00.**

Maxfield Parrish
By Ludwig. 223 pages. 9 x 12. 184 illustrations, 64 in full color. Published at $25.00. Now **$20.00.**

The Great Book of French Impressionism
By Kelder. 448 pages. 12 x 15 1/4. Over 400 illustrations, including 200 full color plates and 16 spectacular full color fold-outs. Huge, exquisitely produced treasury of French Impressionist art, packed with full-page reproductions. Examines the lives and works of all the major Impressionists and Post-Impressionists. Published at $100.00. Now **$59.95.**

Carl Faberge
Goldsmith to the Imperial Court of Russia
By Snowman. 100 page. 8 1/4 x 10 1/2. Over 185 photos, 111 in full color. Originally Published at $35.00. Only **$22.00.**

Contemporary Painting
By Vogt. 135 pages. 7 1/2 x 10 1/2. Over 50 in full color. Penetrating analysis of post World War II European and American art. Including paintings by Jaspar Johns. Andy Warhol, Roy Lichtenstein, Jackson Pollock, others. $19.95. Now **$14.95.**

Twentieth Century Masters of Erotic Art
By Smith. 212 pages. 9 x 12. 190 full color plates presents erotic works by such top-ranking artists as Picasso, Dali, Ernst, Rauschenberg, Rivers. Warhol, and others, many of which have never been displayed in public exhibitions. Only **$25.00.**

Leonardo Da Vinci
538 page. 11 x 14 1/2. Huge. 1,635 illustrations including many large full color plates. Originally published in Italy by the Instituto Geografico De Agostini, this new edition is the most lavish, authoritative ever produced. Published at $60.00. Only **$50.00.**

Rembrandt Paintings
By Gerson. 527 pages 11 x 14 1/2. Huge. Over 730 illustrations, including many large full color plates. Complete, authoritative and beautiful presentation of the great master's work. Written by one of the world's foremost Rembrandt authorities. The book was thirty years in the making in Amsterdam, and is lavishly illustrated with spectacular reproductions. Published at $60.00. Only **$50.00.**

English Cameo Glass
By Grover. 480 pages. 8 x 11. A wealth of rare first-hand material and over 1,000 color and black and white plates makes this book an invaluable reference. Published at $50.00. Now **$30.00.**

20,000 Years of World Painting
By Jaffe. 416 pages. 9 x 13. Historical survey from early to modern art. 1,000 reproductions in full color. Was $50.00. Now **$19.95.**

Stained Glass
By Seddon & Stephens. 205 pages. 473 full color photos. 11 x 14. Covers stained glass from the beginning to the present. Was $39.95 Now **$19.95.**

The Complete Book of Erotic Art
By Allen. More than 300 Paintings and Drawings. Over 100 in full color. Many never before reproduced. 9 x 12. Originally Published at $29.95. Now **$19.95.**

Collecting Political Americana
By Schrade. 93 illustrations. 40 hand tipped plates in color. First major survey on the subject in English. Rare out of print. 137 pages. Only **$25.00.**

Diamonds
By McCracken. A biography and picture gallery of the dean of Indian painters. 170 color and black and white illustrations. He lived and worked among 48 Indian tribes. Catlin's paintings are authentic depictions of daily life of the native Americans. 9 x 11. Out of print. **$18.50.**

The Great Book of Jewels
By Rawls. 488 pages. 11 3/4 x 15 format. Over 400 large reproductions, including over 300 full color plates. Presents the largest number of Currier & Ives prints ever reproduced in a single volume. Huge. Published at $100.00. Only **$55.00.**

Reference Art Books   Phone TOLL-FREE 1-800-238-8288

Putting Your Knowledge to Work

Correspondence (Original)

Even the simplest desktop publishing techniques can greatly improve letters to selected recipients.

When a normal typewritten message crams too many words on one page, an alternate typeface and size can solve the problem.

Deep indention is replaced by narrower columns of "highlights."

Wide columns have been narrowed to increase white space and mitigate eye fatigue.

Careful selection and manipulation of typefaces and sizes can avoid a "gray" look that implies poor organization and discourages readership.

THE WOODEN BOAT SHOW

The Wooden Boat Show in Newport, Rhode Island is the largest show of its kind in the country. Ten thousand qualified showgoers and hundreds of exhibitors attend this show each year. Undoubtedly, it is one of the most important events of the wooden boat industry.

The Wooden Boat Show is the ideal chance for you to reach your audience and to increase your sales. The 1987 show, August 27 - 30, will be our biggest and best one yet. The following are some of the changes we have made to ensure this:

o   Layout

We have added a small boatbuilder's section located near the main gate with excellent visibility to Newport's America's Cup Avenue. Please note that the cost for exhibiting in this section will be based on only the amount of space utilized and not on designated 10 X 20 or 20 X 20 blocks.

o   Exhibitor's Breakfast with a presentation by Jon Wilson, Editor & Publisher of WoodenBoat Magazine.

On Friday August 28, at 8am, Jon will be speaking to all interested exhibitors on the market outlook for wooden boats. There will also be a question/answer period immediately following the discussion. Further information about the presentation will be mailed later.

o   Advertising/Public Relations

We will be increasing our advertising and publicity campaign in order to broaden our pre-show coverage while still attracting the very unique wooden boat attendee.

The enclosed package contains all the necessary information pertaining to exhibiting in this year's show. Please take the time to review the materials and return them as soon as possible. If you have any questions on the forms or the show itself, please don't hesitate to call.

I look forward to working with you on a quality and successful Wooden Boat Show.

Best regards,

Abby Murphy
Show Manager

P.O. BOX 549, NEWPORT, RHODE ISLAND 02840   (401) 846-1600

Correspondence (Makeover)

As word processing programs carry more desktop publishing features, simple use of basic type and design tools can make personal correspondence more readable.

To unify the letterhead, the illustration has been moved to the left and integrated with the address.

A "Dear Wooden Boat Lovers" salutation adds warmth and formally introduces the letter.

A highly readable Times Roman serif typeface has been chosen.

Boldfaced type contrasts subheads with body copy.

The copy for indented sections is set smaller, with reduced leading.

The letter ends by returning to a single wide column that matches the introductory paragraphs.

THE WOODEN BOAT SHOW

P.O. BOX 549, NEWPORT, RHODE ISLAND 02840 (401) 846-1600

Dear Wooden Boat Enthusiast,

The Wooden Boat Show in Newport, Rhode Island is the largest show of its kind in the country. Ten thousand qualified showgoers and hundreds of exhibitors attend this show each year. Undoubtedly, it is one of the most important events of the wooden boat industry.

The Wooden Boat Show is the ideal chance for you to reach your audience and to increase your sales. The 1987 show, August 27 - 30, will be our biggest and best one yet. The following are some of the changes we have made to ensure this:

Layout

We have added a small boatbuilder's section located near the main gate with excellent visibility to Newport's America's Cup Avenue. Please note that the cost for exhibiting in this section will be based on *only* the amount of space utilized and not on designated 10 x 20 or 20 x 20 blocks.

Exhibitor's Breakfast

On Friday August 28, at 8am, Jon Wilson, Editor & Publishers of *Wooden Boat Magazine*, will be speaking to all interested exhibitors on the market outlook for wooden boats. There will also be a question/answer period immediately following the discussion. Further information about the presentation will be mailed later.

Advertising/Public Relations

We will be increasing our advertising and publicity campaign in order to broaden our pre-show coverage while still attracting the very unique wooden boat attendee.

The enclosed package contains all the necessary information pertaining to exhibiting in this year's show. Please take the time to review the materials and return them as soon as possible. If you have any questions on the forms or the show itself, please don't hesitate to call.

I look forward to working with you on a successful Wooden Boat Show.

Best regards,

Abby Murphy
Show Manager

Flyers (Original)

The next four pages show how two similar "question and answer" motifs are manipulated to produce different, yet satisfactory, results.

Only artwork that furthers the communicating power of the brochure should be included. Thus, the question marks have been omitted because the headline and content clearly communicate the "Q&A" format.

Similarly, the illustrations have been omitted to permit larger type and more white space.

Answers beginning with a single, boldface word (e.g., "Yes!") now appear as normal body copy, to heighten the contrast between questions and answers.

Answers to Questions Frequently Asked about Tri-Steel Homes

1. What is the Tri-Steel concept and why is it different from conventional wood frame construction?

The Tri-Steel concept is based upon the utilization and superior quality and strength of steel to form the "frame" or "shell" of a home. This allows the home to be "stick built" on site, but with steel instead of wood and with bolts and fasteners instead of nails and staples.

The superior strength of steel means that frame spacing can be on 6-foot and 8-foot centers instead of 16-inch and 24-inch centers. Plus, we can utilize 9 inches of insulation on the sides and also provide consistent quality, less maintenance, and much greater strength than is possible with conventional construction. In addition, this gives you much greater flexibility inside the home since none of the walls need to be load bearing. **Also important, the entire shell can often be dried-in within 4 to 5 days by an inexperienced crew.**

2. How are Tri-Steel homes unique?

Our homes utilize an engineered and computer designed steel structural system. You can choose from a wide selection of contemporary slant wall designs which stand out among conventional wooden structures or numerous conventional-looking straight wall designs ranging from conservatively gabled roof lines to ultra-modern units allowing clerestory window placement.

3. What are some of the advantages of Tri-Steel homes?

Tri-Steel homes can cost less to erect and can go up much faster. They are exceptionally energy efficient, require almost no exterior maintenance, and are tremendously flexible in their design. In addition to these areas of savings, they offer the strength and durability of steel to withstand extreme weather conditions, termites and fire. The quality of steel is consistently high. Pre-engineered framing components ensure your home goes up one way — **the RIGHT way!** Special snow or wind loads are possible with very little extra cost. They also meet Seismic 4 earthquake specifications - the highest rating required.

4. Have these homes been tried and proven?

Absolutely! In terms of the history of home building, Tri-Steel homes are a new and unique concept; however, these homes have been in use throughout the South for over ten years. Tri-Steel has thousands of structures all across the nation and we are constantly receiving letters from satisfied homeowners attesting to the beauty, strength and energy savings of Tri-Steel structures.

5. Can I put up one of these homes myself and is construction assistance available?

Yes! The home is actually designed to be constructed independently by the buyer. No heavy lifting equipment or special tools are required. The steel beams are designed to bolt together — A to B, B to C — with prepunched holes so you are basically working with a giant erector set. No cutting or welding is required on the job site and complete instructions and drawings are included with the package. Tri-Steel can provide your choice of construction assistance. As part of the assistance available, we can consult with you over the phone, have your shell erected, or provide on-site supervision on a daily or weekly basis.

6. How much flexibility do I have in choosing a home size?

Infinite! A virtually unlimited variety of home sizes are offered from 800 square feet on up. Our homes come in one, two or three level designs with slant or straight walls. We have hundreds of plans drawn and available for immediate mailing and we can also draw custom designs to meet virtually any floor plan or size requirements.

7. Can I add to the home at a later date?

Yes! Additional space may be added in the future at low cost and relative ease allowing you to enlarge your home economically as your needs and income requires.

Flyers (Makeover)

An informative "magazine-style" format has been chosen, which employs creative type treatments to lure the reader into the piece.

Drop caps further contrast questions and answers to create visual tension that holds reader interest.

The Tri-Steel logo area has been made larger and more readable.

Q&A

QUESTIONS AND ANSWERS ABOUT TRI-STEEL HOMES

1 What is the Tri-Steel concept and why is it different from conventional wood frame construction?

The Tri-Steel concept is based upon the utilization and superior quality and strength of steel to form the "frame" or "shell" of a home. This allows the home to be "stick built" on site, but with steel instead of wood and with bolts and fasteners instead of nails and staples.

The superior strength of steel means that frame spacing can be on 6-foot and 8-foot centers instead of 16-inch and 24-inch centers. Plus, we can utilize 9 inches of insulation on the sides and also provide consistent quality, less maintenance, and much greater strength than is possible with conventional construction. In addition, this gives you much greater flexibility inside the home since none of the walls need to be load bearing. Also important, the entire shell can often be dried-in within 4 to 5 days by an inexperienced crew.

2 How are Tri-Steel homes unique?

Our homes utilize an engineered and computer designed steel structural system. You can choose from a wide selection of contemporary slant wall designs which stand out among conventional wooden structures or numerous conventional-looking straight wall designs ranging from conservatively gabled roof lines to ultra-modern units allowing clerestory window placement.

3 What are some of the advantages of Tri-Steel homes?

Tri-Steel homes can cost less to erect and can go up much faster. They are exceptionally energy efficient, require almost no exterior maintenance, and are tremendously flexible in their design. In addition to these areas of savings, they offer the strength and durability of steel to withstand extreme weather conditions, termites and fire. The quality of steel is consistently high. Pre-engineered framing components ensure your home goes up one way - the RIGHT way! Special snow or wind loads are possible with very little extra cost. They also meet Seismic 4 earthquake specifications - the highest rating required.

4 Have these homes been tried and proven?

Absolutely! In terms of the history of home building, Tri-Steel homes are a new and unique concept. However, these homes have been in use throughout the South for over ten year. Tri-Steel has thousands of structures all across the nation and we are constantly receiving letters from satisfied homeowners attesting to the beauty, strength and energy savings of Tri-Steel structures.

5 Can I put up one of these homes myself and is construction assistance available?

Yes! The home is actually designed to be constructed independently by the buyer. No heavy lifting equipment or special tools are required. The steel beams are designed to bolt together - A to B, B to C - with prepunched holes so you are basically working with a giant erector set. No cutting or welding is required on the job site and complete instructions and drawings are included with the package. Tri-Steel can provide your choice of construction assistance. As part of the assistance available, we can consult with you over the phone, have your shell erected, or provide on-site supervision on a daily or weekly basis.

6 How much flexibility do I have in choosing a home size?

Infinite! A virtually unlimited variety of home sizes are offered from 800 square feet on up. Our homes come in one, two or three level designs with slant or straight walls. We have hundreds of plans drawn and available for immediate mailing and we can also draw custom designs to meet virtually any floor plan or size requirements.

7 Can I add to the home at a later date?

Yes! Additional space may be added in the future at low cost and relative ease allowing you to enlarge your home economically as your needs and income requires.

Tri-Steel Structures

5800 Campus Circle Irving, TX 75063
(214) 580-3400
© 1987, All Rights Reserved

Putting Your Knowledge to Work

Flyers (Original)

Too much copy crammed into a small space creates a "dark" look that discourages readership.

Questions set in bold, upper-case type are difficult to read.

Similarly, answers are difficult to read because long lines aren't compensated by increased type size and leading.

A three-column format has been chosen, with questions (shorter than the body copy) appearing in the narrow left-hand column.

Justified type has been used in the original document, creating exaggerated word spacing. Often, a widow appears on the second line.

THE MOST FREQUENTLY ASKED QUESTIONS ABOUT A SPORT IT DEALERSHIP

1. **WHAT IS THE INITIAL INVESTMENT FOR A SPORT IT DEALERSHIP?**

   $1,500.

2. **IS THERE A ROYALTY OR SERVICE FEE?**

   There is no royalty fee, however, there is a minimal $25.00 service fee to cover the following: monthly newsletters, toll free consultation service and on-going research for obtaining new suppliers. This $25.00 service fee is due the 10th of each month and can not fluctuate during the five year term of the Sport It Dealer Agreement.

3. **ARE THERE ANY OTHER FEES OR CHARGES?**

   Yes. There is a $100.00 renewal fee at the end of the five year term of the Agreement which will renew the Agreement for an additional five year period. Also, if you elect to sell your dealership or transfer to a new location a $100.00 transfer fee is needed to cover the cost of changes and modifications to our records, files, et cetera.

4. **WHAT QUALIFICATIONS ARE NEEDED TO BECOME A SPORT IT DEALER?**

   The Sport It Home Office receives over 1,600 inquiries per month. From these inquiries nearly 400 applications are received. The evaluation committee selects approximately 40 applicants that will become Sport It Dealers. These applicants must have a good credit standing, positive references and have potential to represent Sport It as professional dealers.

5. **WHAT DO I RECEIVE FOR MY INITIAL INVESTMENT OF $1,500?**

   The initial $1,500 investment provides you with a business opportunity allowing immediate access to brand name merchandise at very competitive prices which would not be available to you as an independent dealer. The Sport It Dealership puts you in business immediately. You will receive catalogs, price lists, purchase order forms, an Operations Manual and miscellaneous samples in your initial box of materials.

6. **WHAT IS THE TERM OF THE SPORT IT DEALERSHIP AGREEMENT?**

   Five years.

7. **MAY I HAVE A PARTNER OR PARTNERS WITH MY SPORT IT DEALERSHIP?**

   Yes. You may have as many partners as you wish.

8. **ARE THERE ANY TAX ADVANTAGES WITH MY SPORT IT DEALERSHIP?**

   There are many tax advantages available for your home operated business. A portion of your rent, house payment, electricity, heat, insurance, taxes, et cetera, can be used as deductions. In addition, automobile expenses and depreciation may be deducted according to the percentage that your vehicle is used for business.

9. **CAN I FINANCE MY INITIAL INVESTMENT OF $1,500?**

   The initial $1,500 investment can be charged to your MasterCard or Visa credit card enabling you to make monthly payments for your Sport it Dealership.

10. **CAN I SELL MY SPORT IT DEALERSHIP?**

    Yes. Some Dealers, due to unforeseen circumstances, have had to sell their Dealership. Most Dealers, who have sold their Dealership have done so at a substantial profit.

Flyers (Makeover)

A staggered three-column format clearly separates questions and answers, allowing the reader to pick and choose specific areas of interest.

A "friendlier" typeface has been chosen, set ragged right.

SPORT IT

The Most Frequently Asked Questions About A Sport It Dealership

1. **Is there a royalty or service fee?**

   There is no royalty fee, however, there is a minimal $25.00 service fee to cover the following: monthly newsletters, toll free consultation service and on-going research for obtaining new suppliers. This $25.00 service fee is due the 10th of each month and can not fluctuate during the five year term of the Sport It Dealer Agreement.

2. **What is the initial investment for a Sport It Dealership?**

   $1,500.

3. **Are there any other fees?**

   Yes. There is a $100.00 renewal fee at the end of the five year term of the Agreement which will renew the Agreement for an additional five year period. Also, if you elect to sell your dealership or transfer to a new location a $100.00 transfer fee is needed to cover the cost of changes and modifications to our records, files, et cetera.

4. **What qualifications are needed to become a Sport It Dealer?**

   The Sport It Home Office receives over 1,600 inquiries per month. From these inquiries nearly 400 applications are received. The evaluation committee selects approximately 40 applicants that will become Sport It Dealers. These applicants must have a good credit standing, positive references and have potential to represent Sport It as professional dealers.

5. **What do I receive for my initial investment of $1,500?**

   The initial $1,500 investment provides you with a business opportunity allowing immediate access to brand name merchandise at very competitive prices which would not be available to you as an independent dealer. The Sport It Dealership puts you in business immediately. You will receive catalogs, prices lists, purchase order forms, Operations Manual and miscellaneous sample merchandise in your initial box of materials.

6. **What is the term of the Sport It Dealership Agreement?**

   Five years.

7. **May I have a partner or partners with my Sport It Dealership?**

   Yes. You may have as many partners as you wish.

8. **Are there any tax advantages with my Sport It Dealership?**

   There are many tax advantages available for your home operated business. A portion of your rent, house payment, electricity, heat, insurance, taxes, et cetera can be used as deductions. In addition, automobile expenses and depreciation may be deducted according to the percentage that your vehicle is used for business.

9. **Can I finance my initial investment of $1,500?**

   The initial $1,500 investment can be charged to your MasterCard or Visa credit card enabling you to make monthly payments for your Sport It Dealership.

Shorter lines and narrower columns make the answers more readable.

Putting Your Knowledge to Work

User Manuals (Original)

Because of their timeliness and design simplicity, user guides, reference manuals and technical documentation are ideal for desktop publishing. Note how a few simple modifications vastly improve the Crest Fan user manual.

The abrupt, military-like copy ("Read and Save These Instructions") is replaced by a friendlier and more informative "How to Install Your New Crest Fan."

The "UL Approved" symbol, a visual distraction, also has been reduced in size—by the time the customer reads an instruction book, the "selling job" has been done!

The "Code #," primarily an internal document tracking number, has been moved from the front cover. Such identifiers should be placed in small type on the last page of documents.

Code # T-1

CREST

READ AND SAVE THESE INSTRUCTIONS

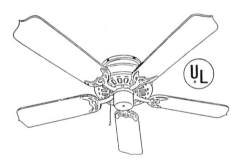

These instructions are intended for use with the following
U.L. Listed Crest models.

SERIES: MODELS:
4000   *04-002 Through 04-498

4500   *04-502 Through 04-698

*Includes only those models which end in even numbers.

We thank you for selecting one of our products to make your house a home. We dedicate considerable time to insure that our products provide high quality and the highest level of customer satisfaction. If, however, problems should arise, please keep your bill of sale as proof of purchase.

24.

User Manuals (Makeover)

Note how few simple modifications have made this document more inviting and readable.

The illustration has been touched up and screened, enhancing its impact and adding contrast to the surrounding white space.

Series and model numbers are set closer together at the upper right-hand corner of the page, allowing readers to quickly identify appropriate models.

The Crest logo is moved to a bottom corner, where readers are accustomed to finding such information.

A small, informative table of contents adds balance to the introductory paragraph and acts as a quick reference.

HOW TO INSTALL YOUR NEW CREST FAN

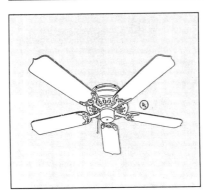

These instructions are intended for use with the following U.L. Listed Crest models. Save this manual for future reference.

Series: **4000**
Models: **04-001** through **04-499**

Series:**4500**
Models: **04-501** through **40-699**

TABLE OF CONTENTS:

We thank you for selecting one of our porducts to make your house a home. We dedicate considerable time to insure that our products provide high quality and the highest level of customer satisfaction. If, however, problems should arise, please keep your bill of sale as proof of purchase.

CREST

Putting Your Knowledge to Work

User Manuals (Original)

On the inside pages, a few minor changes have dramatically improved the readability and appeal of the piece.

Horizontal rules have been thickened to match type size.

Long columns of type have been narrowed to enhance readability.

GENERAL

1. To ensure the success of the installation, be sure to read the instructions and review the diagrams throughly before beginning. Review and follow only the instructions that are applicable for your fan.

2. All electrical connections must be in accordance with local codes, ordinances, or National Electrical Code. If you are unfamiliar with methods of installing electrical wiring, secure the services of a qualified electrician.

3. Make sure that your installation site will not allow rotating fan blades to come in contact with any object. A minimum clearance of 7 feet from the floor to the trailing edge of the blade is required.

4. If you are installing more than one ceiling fan, make sure that you do not mix fan blade sets.

5. If the fan will be mounted on a ceiling outlet box, a 4" x 2¼" deep metal octagon outlet box is required. The outlet box must be directly supported by the building structure. The outlet box and its support must be able to support the moving weight of the fan (at least 50 lbs.) The outlet box must not twist or work loose. Do not use plastic outlet boxes! The mounting bracket must be attached using the hardware supplied with the ceiling outlet box.

6. If mounting fan to a joist, the joist must be able to support the moving weight of the fan (at least 50 lbs.)

7. Installation to a concrete ceiling should be performed by a qualified electrician.

8. Before beginning, disconnect power by removing fuse or turning off circuit breaker.

9. After the fan is completely installed, make sure that all connections are secure to prevent fan from falling.

10. Do not insert anything into fan blades while ceiling fan is operating.

11. Fan must be turned off and stopped before reversing fan direction.

NOTE: The important safeguards and instructions appearing in this manual are not meant to cover all possible conditions and situations that may occur. It must be understood that common sense, caution and care are factors which cannot be built into any product. These factors must be supplied by the person(s) caring for and operating the unit.

TOOLS AND MATERIALS REQUIRED

. Philips screw driver
. Blade screw driver
. Adjustable wrench
. Step ladder
. Wire cutters
. Wiring supplies as required by electrical code

CAUTION: Before assembling your ceiling fan, refer to sections titled MOUNTING OPTIONS and ELECTRICAL CONNECTIONS. If you feel you do not have electrical wiring knowledge or experience, refer to a do-it-yourself wiring handbook or have your fan installed by a licensed electrician.

2

User Manuals (Makeover)

With body copy, illustrations and caution notes organized into a consistent format, the customer can read the document with far less effort.

Subheads are now set flush-left (flush-right on right-hand pages) so readers can thumb through the manual and quickly spot major information categories.

The "tools and materials" illustration has been moved to the top and screened to call immediate attention to required items.

Skillful manipulation of type and illustrations allows you to place more information on each page.

GENERAL

1. To ensure the success of the installation, be sure to read the instructions and review the diagrams thoroughly before beginning. Review and follow only the instructions that are applicable for your fan.
2. All electrical connections must be in accordance with local codes, ordinances, or National Electrical Code. If you are unfamiliar with methods of installing electrical wiring, secure the services of a qualified electrician.
3. Make sure that your installation site will not allow rotating fan blades to come in contact with any object. A minimum clearance of 7 feet from the floor to the trailing edge of the blade is required.
4. If you are installing more than one ceiling fan, make sure that you do not mix fan blade sets.
5. If the fan will be mounted on a ceiling outlet box, a 4" x 2 1/8" deep metal octagon outlet box is required. The outlet box must be directly supported by the building structure. The outlet box and its support must be able to support the moving weight of the fan (at least 50 lbs.) The outlet box must not twist or work loose. Do not use plastic outlet boxes! The mounting bracket must be attached using the hardware supplied with the ceiling outlet box.
6. If mounting fan to a joist, the joist must be able to support the moving weight of the fan (at least 50 lbs.).
7. Installation to a concrete ceiling should be performed by a qualified electrician.
8. Before beginning, disconnect power by removing fuse or turning off circuit breaker.
9. After the fan is completely installed, make sure that all connections are secure to prevent fan from falling.
10. Do not insert anything into fan blades while ceiling fan is operating.
11. Fan must be turned off and stopped before reversing fan direction.
12. This fan is not intended to be supported by single threaded J-Hook supports.

NOTE: The important safe guards and instructions appearing in this manual are not meant to cover all possible conditions and situations that may occur. It must be understood that common sense, caution and care are factors which cannot be built into any product. These factors must be supplied by the person(s) caring for and operating the unit.

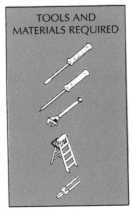

TOOLS AND MATERIALS REQUIRED

CAUTION: Before assembling your ceiling fan refer to sections titled MOUNTING OPTIONS and ELECTRICAL CONNECTIONS. If you feel you do not have electrical wiring knowledge or experience, refer to a do-it-yourself wiring handbook or have your fan installed by a licensed electrician.

UNPACKING THE FAN

Unpack the fan and check contents: You should receive:
☐ Fan motor assembly
☐ Downrod assembly
☐ Canopy
☐ Blade set
☐ Blade attachment flange
☐ Package of hardware for mounting blades
☐ Mounting bracket and hardware
☐ Wire nuts for electrical connection
☐ Wooden tassel

• Some models have these parts factory assembled

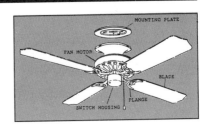

Advertisements (Original)

Parallelism can easily lead to confusion. In this ad, three disparate and confusing messages often repeat information and tend to confuse the reader.

Three repeating headlines waste valuable space and segment the ad unnecessarily.

The headlines from the original ad are retained, but used as subheads for the individual copy blocks.

Phone numbers and hotel information are repeated throughout the piece, creating mental "clutter."

Advertisements (Makeover)

The ad is strengthened considerably by modifying headlines and body copy to present a coherent message.

A single "master headline" now dominates the page, with reinforcing subheads placed immediately below.

The original illustrations are reduced and repositioned.

Runaround type effectively ties body copy to illustrations.

The bottom of the ad has been cleaned up and the response vehicle— Yosemite's Holiday Hotline phone number—is now a dominant visual element.

Newsletters (Original)

This piece demonstrates how design principles applied inappropriately can result in a poorly designed document.

The rules in the body copy tend to fight with the illustration box and rules in the masthead.

Nonproportional typefaces create uneven word spacing.

Indention within narrow columns often causes awkward blocks of white space.

Technology Today

LOUISIANA TRANSPORTATION RESEARCH CENTER

Vol. 3 No. 1   January 1987

RESEARCH PROFILES

NEW METHOD STUDIED FOR BRIDGE REPAIRS

One of the most common forms of damage to the superstructure of steel bridges results from vehicle impact. This damage rarely causes a bridge to collapse, but results in the serious weakening of the structure as such damage accumulates. Member replacement is an expensive repair, and thus a more economical alternative has been needed.

Heat straightening offers the potential for quick and effective repairs for bent steel members. LSU has just completed the first phase of a research project on heat straightening under the sponsorship of LTRC. The process of heat straightening consists of heating the bent member at appropriate locations such that during the cooling process the unequal shrinkage will induce thermal stresses that straighten the member. The few experts who currently employ this technique base the process on experience. The research project will develop a rational methodology for determining the type, number and location of heat application points required to straighten damaged members. The specific objectives of this research project are:

Phase 1 : Analytical and experimental evaluation of heat straightening techniques in the laboratory.

Phase 2 : Field evaluation of heat straightening techniques and development of an interactive program for automated design of the repair scheme.

Phase 3 : Documentation and training sessions for La. DOTD personnel.

The information obtained in phase one of this project is available upon request from LTRC.

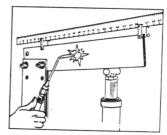

HEATING LABORATORY SAMPLE

STUDY UNDERWAY ON EMBANKMENT FAILURES

An in-house study on slope rehabilitation is moving forward in an effort to find an economical solution to a problem that has troubled the department for more than a decade--failing slopes on man-made embankments, particularly along the Interstate system.

Five failed slopes are being rehabilitated under the project, using three different methods: injection of lime and lime-fly ash; rebuilding with lime-

Newsletters (Makeover)

Contrasting typefaces and rules give the piece the contemporary feel appropriate to a technology newsletter.

The masthead has been completely reworked (see page 114).

A highly readable Times Roman typeface contrasts the sans-serif headline.

The caption is moved inside the illustration for better balance.

A 20% screen behind the illustration adds contrast and balances the bold masthead with the copy.

TECHNOLOGY
TODAY

A quarterly publication of the Louisiana Transportation Research Center

Summer 1987   Vol. 3, No. 3   *LTRC*

Research Profiles

New Method Studied for Bridge Repairs

One of the most common forms of damage to the superstructure of steel bridges results from vehicle impact. This damage rarely causes a bridge to collapse, but results in the serious weakening of the structure as such damage accumulates. Member replacement is an expensive repair, and thus a more economical alternative has been needed.

Heat straightening offers the potential for quick and effective repairs for bent steel members. LSU has just completed the first phase of a research project on heat straightening under the sponsorship of LTRC. The process of heat straightening consists of heating the bent member at appropriate locations such that during the cooling process the unequal shrinkage will induce thermal stresses that straighten the member. The few experts who currently employ this technique base the process on experience. The research project will develop a rational methodology for determining the type, number and location of heat application points required to straighten damaged members. The specific objectives of this research project are:

Phase 1: Analytical and experimental evaluation of heat straightening techniques in the laboratory.

Phase 2: Field evaluation of heat straightening techniques and development of an interactive

program for automated design of the repair scheme.

Phase 3: Documentation and training sessions for La. DOTD personnel.

The information obtained in phase one of this project is available upon request from LTRC.

Study Underway on Embankment Failures

An in-house study on slope rehabilitation is moving forward in an effort to find an economical solution

to a problem that has troubled the department for more than a decade—failing slopes on man-made embankments, particularly along the Interstate system.

Five failed slopes are being rehabilitated under the project, using three different methods: injection of lime and lime-fly ash; rebuilding with lime treated, compacted lifts; and reinforcement with geogrid. Construction is essentially complete on three study slopes on I-20 district 04 (Monroe), and a fourth slope is underway on I-210 in district 07 (Lake Charles). A fifth slope on I-20 in district 04 is still to be let to

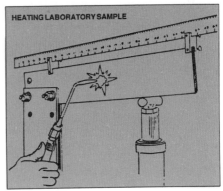

HEATING LABORATORY SAMPLE

Newsletters (Original)

In-house newsletters and other time-sensitive documents often can be made more appealing at no additional cost.

Headlines "butt" each other at the top, creating too much uniformity and symmetry.

A lack of indention sets up a uniformity that leads to boredom when the readers' eyes aren't challenged by contrast.

Matching type styles in headlines and body copy create a "gray" look.

Similarly, the lack of contrast caused by large square blocks of copy and excessive leading between paragraphs causes readers to lose interest.

COMPUTER CENTER
FACULTY BULLETIN

CALIFORNIA STATE UNIVERSITY, NORTHRIDGE   OCTOBER 1985

WHATEVER HAPPENED TO COMPUTER AIDED INSTRUCTION

by Kurt Webb

Computer Aided Instruction (CAI) had its moments in the sun several years ago and has since seemed to have faded from the academic computing scene. However, there are now indications that a resurgence in CAI is occurring. This renaissance may be due to two factors: (1) The increased availability of authoring systems on micros and mainframe computers; and (2) The increased awareness and utilization of computing among educators.

An authoring system is a software product that allows the educator: (1) to organize the subject material, to be presented to the student, in a systematic way; (2) to query the student taking the computerized lessons on their comprehension of the subject material; (3) to review the material previously presented or continue on with new material depending on how the student responded to the queries; and (4) to analyze student response to the lesson as a whole to help determine the next step in the learning process. Once such a CAI lesson has been prepared by using an authoring system, it can be presented to any number of students with each student taking the lesson at their convenience and at their own pace.

The Computer Center has recently purchased two authoring systems for the IBM PC. These are TENCORE and the McGraw-Hill Authoring System. These two systems do require that the author as well as students have access to IBM PC computers. A third authoring, Instructional Workbench, is available on the AT&T 3B5 mainframe computers. These computers can be accessed from virtually any terminal on campus.

More on CAI and authoring systems will be forthcoming. In the meantime, if you are interested in any of these products contact Kurt Webb at Extension 3966.

MICROCOMPUTER JOURNAL FOR INSTRUCTIONAL USERS

by J. S. Fleming

COLLEGIATE MICROCOMPUTER is "a quarterly journal devoted to all aspects of microcomputers in the higher education curricula." A sample copy received by the Computer Center included articles such as "The Use of Microcomputers in the Teaching of Calculus," "An Introductory Course in System Dynamics," "Using Microcomputers to Store and Evaluate Exam Items," and "Computer Literacy for Undergraduate Humanities and Social Majors."

If interested, this journal is published by COLLEGIATE MICROCOMPUTER, Rose-Hulman Institute of Technology, Terre Haute, IN 47803. Individual subscriptions are $28.00. A sample copy may be reviewed at the Computer Center, Engineering 121.

MICROCOMPUTER GRAPHICS BEGIN TO GROW UP

by Dave Crawford

Do you remember what life was like before computer graphics?

If you are old enough to be reading this you probably do, since computer graphics for popular consumption have been with us for only a few years. But computer-generated pictures have become so common in movies and on television that most of us no longer marvel at them. We accept them unthinkingly, as if they had always been with us.

We watch science fiction movies in which vivid alien landscapes have been created in a computer's memory without using models of any kind. We are perfectly accustomed to music videos in

Newsletters (Makeover)

Creative use of white space, indention and leading helps make the piece more readable.

A simple, appealing masthead often is the best way to improve a newsletter or tabloid.

Rules between columns and in the margins tie the masthead to the body copy.

Boldface characters at beginnings of paragraphs provide contrast without the intricacies of drop caps.

A "rag bottom" format permits design flexibility and saves production time.

Faculty BULLETIN

Computer Center
California State University, Northridge   November 1985

Whatever Happened to Computer Aided Instruction

Computer Aided Instruction (CAI) had its moments in the sun several years ago and has since seemed to have faded from the academic computing scene. However, there are now indications that a resurgence in CAI is occurring. This renaissance may be due to two factors: (1) The increased availability of authoring systems on micros and mainframe computers; and (2) The increased awareness and utilization of computing among educators.

An authoring system is a software product that allows the educator: (1) to organize the subject material, to be presented to the student, in a systematic way; (2) to query the student taking the computerized lessons on their comprehension of the subject material; (3) to review the material previously presented or continue on with new material depending on how the student responded to the queries; and (4) to analyze student response to the lesson to help determine the next step in the learning process. Once such a CAI lesson has been prepared by using an authoring system, it can be presented to any number of students with each student taking the lesson at their convenience and at their own pace.

The Computer Center has recently purchased two authoring systems for the IBM PC. These are TENCORE and the McGraw-Hill Authoring System. These two systems do require that the author as well as the students have access to IBM PC computers. A third authoring, Instructional Workbench, is available on the AT&T 3B5 mainframe computers. These computers can be accessed from virtually any terminal.

More on CAI and authoring systems will be forthcoming. In the meantime, if you are interested in any of these products contact Kurt Webb at Extension 3966.

Microcomputer Journal for Instructional Users

Collegiate Microcomputer is "a quarterly journal devoted to all aspects of microcomputers in the higher education curricula." A sample copy received by the Computer Center included "The Use of Microcomputers in the Teaching of Calculus," "An Introductory Course in System Dynamics," "Using Microcomputers to store and Evaluate Exam Items," and "Computer Literacy for Undergraduate Humanities and Social Majors."

If interested, this journal is published by Collegiate Microcomputer, Rose-Hulman Institute of Technology, Terre Haute, IN 47803. Individual subscriptions are $28.00. A sample copy may be reviewed at the Computer Center. Engineering 121.

Microcomputer Graphics Begin to Grow Up

Do you remember what life was like before computer graphics? If you are old enough to be reading this you probably do, since computer graphics for popular consumption have been with us for only a few years. But computer-generated pictures have become so common in movies and on television that most of us no longer marvel at them. We accept them unthinkingly, as if they had always been with us.

We watch science fiction movies in which vivid alien landscapes have been created in a computer's memory without using models of any kind. We are perfectly accustomed to music videos in

Mastheads

The four illustrations on this spread show how mastheads can be reworked to create the appropriate foundation for a newsletter's content.

The map of Louisiana is too complex and contributes little to the message.

Technology Today

LOUISIANA TRANSPORTATION RESEARCH CENTER

Vol. 3 No. 1   January 1987

RESEARCH PROFILES

NEW METHOD STUDIED FOR BRIDGE REPAIRS

One of the most common forms of damage to the superstructure of steel bridges results from vehicle impact. This damage rarely causes a bridge to

Phase 3 : Documentation and training sessions for La. DOTD personnel.

The information obtained in phase one of this project is available upon request from LTRC.

The archaic typeface doesn't effectively communicate "technology."

An upbeat typeface, contrasted by the bold sans-serif "Today," creates a high-tech flavor.

TECHNOLOGY

TODAY

Summer 1987   Vol. 3, No. 3

A quarterly publication of the Louisiana Transportation Research Center

LTRC

Research Profiles

New Method Studied for Bridge Repairs

One of the most common forms of damage to the superstructure of steel bridges results from vehicle impact.

program for automated design of the repair scheme.

Phase 3: Documentation and training sessions for La. DOTD personnel.

The information obtained in phase one of this project is available upon

to a problem that has troubled the department for more than a decade—failing slopes on man-made embankments, particularly along the Interstate system.

Five failed slopes are being rehabilitated under the project, using

Hairline rules are used sparingly but effectively to tie headlines with supporting copy and logo.

Mastheads

A good masthead is often the best way to improve the look of a newsletter or tabloid.

Simple mastheads are best; the too-bold type set against the horizontal lines creates distraction and fights with body copy.

The subhead is far too large and contributes little to the message.

A narrow, condensed type creates valuable white space around a three-column grid.

The subhead has been eliminated and replaced by the less obtrusive "Restaurant Technology" slugline.

Business Reports (Original)

The low-contrast, "gray" tone of business reports and memos often undercuts the effectiveness of good writing, persuasive argument and strong evidence.

Because busy managers have only a short time to read a great deal of material, a good business document presented with straight typewritten copy is often at a disadvantage.

Although critical to the report, long blocks of supporting evidence tend to discourage readership.

Data presented with uneven spacing jars concentration and indicates poor organization.

the average late riser, this product will revolutionize his or her sleeping habits.

CURRENT SNOOZE ALARM SALES

As stated previously, we believe that a high number of present users of snooze alarm technology will want to own TardiSnooz. Current sales of snooze alarms have never been higher, as the figures below show:

YEAR	# UNITS SOLD	$ RETAIL
1965	1,100	$ 12,000
1970	65,000	430,000
1975	220,000	2,800,000
1980	673,000	5,900,000
1985	1,220,000	11,670,000

A corresponding trend of employee tardiness has become evident, particularly in the last ten years. In fact, some researchers believe that snooze alarms have indeed played a large part in <u>causing</u> employee tardiness. According to Real Life Information in Palo Alto, California, "Snooze alarm technology is largely responsible for the dramatic rise in employee tardiness and late calls. Further, the admonishment thrust upon the average employee, compounded by the guilt, feelings of inadequacy and consequent resentment, creates an unresolved <u>authority-figure conflict</u>, resulting in sharply decreased productivity....One solution to this problem is a mechanism whereby the employee can at least call in late with a feeling of efficiency and accomplishment, instead of languishing in <u>commuter-frustrated dissonance</u> on his or her way to work."

Clearly, the above findings indicate the need for added features to snooze technology. This, coupled with the fall in wholesale modem chip prices, could make TardiSnooz our sale item of the decade.

PROJECTED TARDISNOOZ SALES

Based on a 1,000-piece consumer survey mailed last month (see attached data), we found consumers receptive, and indeed eager, to pay the slightly higher price that TardiSnooz would command. Below are projected sales figures, based on our survey:

PROJECTED TARDISNOOZ SALES

YEAR	# UNITS PROJECTED	$ RETAIL
1990	34,000	$ 430,000
1991	81,000	970,000
1992	239,000 (Break-even)	2,400,000
1993	310,000	3,700,000
1994	228,000 (Recession Projected)	2,200,000
1995	426,000	4,450,000

When you examine the above figures, and consider that all we have to do is add a $.93 modem chip to our present alarms, the conclusion is inescapable to all but the most ardent critics that our company should

Business Reports (Makeover)

Even the most basic layout software allows you to substitute interesting, informative charts, graphs and other visuals for text-based data.

Charts and graphs present information in a digestible, interesting manner.

Research information is broken into several paragraphs and indented left and right for additional emphasis.

the average late riser, this product will revolutionize his or her sleeping habits.

CURRENT SNOOZE ALARM SALES

As stated previously, we believe that a high number of present users of snooze alarm technology will want to own TardiSnooz. Current sales of snooze alarms have never been higher, as the figures below show:

Snooze Alarm Sales 1965 — 1985
(000's)

	$10,000
	$5,000
	$1,000

| 1965 | 1970 | 1975 | 1980 | 1985 |

A corresponding trend of employee tardiness has become evident, particularly in the last ten years. In fact, some researchers believe that snooze alarms have indeed played a large part in causing employee tardiness. According to Real Life Information in Palo Alto, California,

"Snooze alarm technology is largely responsible for the dramatic rise in employee tardiness and late calls. Further, the admonishment thrust upon the average employee, compounded by the guilt, feelings of inadequacy and consequent resentment, creates an unresolved authority-figure conflict, resulting in sharply decreased productivity....

One solution to this problem is a mechanism whereby the employee can at least call in late with a feeling of efficiency and accomplishment, instead of languishing in commuter-frustrated dissonance on his or her way to work."

Clearly, the above findings indicate the need for added features to snooze technology. This, coupled with the fall in wholesale modem chip prices, could make TardiSnooz our sale item of the decade.

Based on a 1,000-piece consumer survey mailed last month (see attached data), we found consumers receptive, and indeed eager, to pay the slightly higher price that TardiSnooz would command. Below are projected sales figures, based on our survey:

Projected TardiSnooze Sales

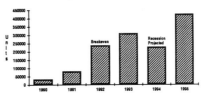

When you examine the above figures, and consider that all we have to do is add a $.93 modem chip to our present alarms, the conclusion is inescapable to all but the most ardent critics that our company should move forward with

Putting Your Knowledge to Work

Charts & Graphs

Quantitive information can be greatly enhanced using visual representations. The illustrations below show four ways the same information can be presented to make data more appealing.

Snooze Alarm Sales 1965 - 1985 (000's)

A three-dimensional effect enhances a basic line graph.

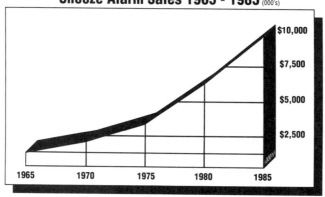

Illustrations within a graph can add humor and further identify the content.

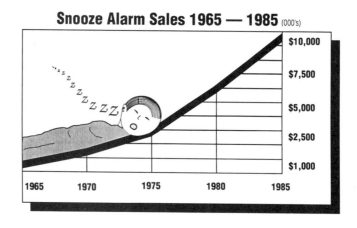

Charts & Graphs

Software is available that formats basic data into charts and graphs. Then you can use your layout software to make revisions and embellishments.

Rules, screens and drop shadows can make a simple bar chart more compelling.

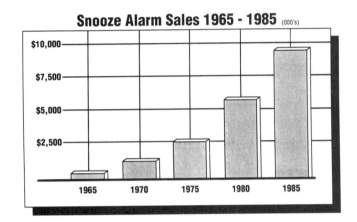

Illustrations that relate to the subject matter can form the dominant visual of a chart or graph.

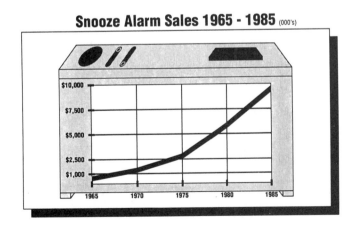

Consistency versus Correctness

Rules are made to be broken.

You may be a bit concerned that the "before-and-after" examples featured in this section break many of the rules and conventions presented in Section One. As mentioned before, there are no universal rules of graphic design, except those of common sense and appropriateness. Design solutions—be they typeface choices, column widths or headline treatments—that work in some situations simply won't work in others.

The goal in Section Two and throughout this book is not to establish rules, but to further your awareness of appropriate and inappropriate ways of applying design basics to your desktop publishing efforts. Although fundamentals should never be completely ignored, good graphic design is largely intuitive. The more responsive you become to your own design sense and intuition, the more you'll develop your own inherent talents.

By now, you should be more comfortable with your ability to use the basic concepts outlined in Section One. No doubt you can see how they've been applied in the real-life examples found in this section. Instead of passively accepting the makeovers and examples in this section as ultimate or definitive design solutions, you may feel motivated to do better.

Take the time now to review those examples and create your own makeovers! You may even want to stop reading at this point, boot up your computer and develop alternative ways of solving the design problems presented in the previous pages.

A Note on Style

Style doesn't emerge overnight, but rather evolves through discipline and hard work.

Style emerges as the way you solve the various design problems that pop up as you become increasingly familiar with the capabilities—and limitations—of your desktop publishing hardware and software.

Your unique graphic design style will evolve in time—as a tool not only for completing specific projects, but also for experimenting and learning.

Remember, desktop publishing gives you unprecedented creative power. In fact, you have more power at your fingertips than any previous generation of graphic designers!

In the past, it would have been prohibitively expensive for a graphic artist to set type and paste up a document simply for learning purposes. Desktop publishing permits you to go through the same learning process at no charge—on the screen of your computer! And if you have access to a laser printer, you can see the tangible results of your efforts for pennies a copy.

When in Doubt Seek Help

By now, you should be turning into something of a critic.

You should have a strong sense of why an ad looks cramped and gray, why a newsletter doesn't look "newsy" or why a business report lacks zest. More important, you should be able to solve basic design problems by applying rules and good old intuition.

Sooner or later, however, you'll no doubt come to a point where you just can't further improve a document—yet it still doesn't look quite right. Don't be afraid to seek professional help. It's always a good idea—and often a necessity—to consult a graphic designer (or other person knowledgeable in design) who can give professional assistance on more complex projects.

For example, design tasks involving logos, mastheads, multiple colors and complex type manipulation often require the consultation of a professional. You may even want to work with a graphic artist to format the basic "look and feel" of all your documents, then fill in copy and artwork according to the designer's specifications.

After reading this book, you'll be able to communicate your

design problem more effectively to a graphic artist, then work with the artist to find a satisfactory solution.

Moving On

Now that you're acquainted with the basics of graphic design and know how those elements work together to produce successful design solutions, you'll no doubt want to begin work on a specific project. Section Three covers several major design categories and presents valuable tips and tricks for producing specific documents.

SECTION THREE

Getting Down to Business

Chapter 7: Developing a Format & Style

Desktop publishing moves you beyond the constraints of traditional type-setting and paste-up methods.

Let's continue to explore practical design for desktop publishing by taking a close look at various types of projects you're likely to produce. In this section, you'll learn some of the tips and techniques experienced desktop publishers use when producing specific types of print communications. In addition, you'll see how desktop publishing quickly moves you beyond the constraints of traditional typesetting and paste-up methods.

The following chapters address design and page layout for newsletters, catalogs, tabloids, advertisements, brochures, books and stationery.

Those categories barely scratch the surface of what you can produce with desktop publishing. Many creative professionals also use desktop publishing programs to prepare presentations–slides and overhead transparencies, for example. Others use it for simple projects such as price lists and press releases.

Formats define the placement of margins, borders and other elements repeated on every page.

Before examining those specific subject areas, let's look at some design considerations common to all those categories.

Consistency and Efficiency

Central to desktop publishing's power is its ability to create templates, or a permanent framework, based on formats that can be repeated from project to project.

Most desktop publishing programs make it easy to establish formats and store them as templates.

Formats

Many desktop publishing programs allow you to establish master page layouts, usually referred to as "master" or "default" pages, based on the format you create.

Formats define the placement of margins, borders, columns, rules, headlines, titles, page numbers and other elements repeated on every page.

Templates

Templates carry the idea of formats even further.

Templates speed up the production cycle and help maintain consistency.

Templates provide a framework for a format to be used from project to project. When you've formatted the first issue of your newsletter, for example, subsequent issues are much easier to produce because they can be built on the framework of the original issue.

Likewise, once you've established a "look" for your newspaper advertisements, week-to-week product and price changes can be easily executed without having to start from scratch each time.

Thus, templates speed up the production cycle and help maintain consistency. In addition, they add a "family resemblance" to your ads and publications, thereby increasing their effectiveness.

Templates are easy to create. When you open a previously saved desktop publishing file, most desktop publishing programs prompt you to choose between "Open Original" or "Open Copy." When you open a copy of the file, the original stays intact, allowing you to create a stable of ready-to-complete "empty" advertisements, brochures or newsletters.

Likewise, when saving a file, you have the alternative of saving it under its original name or creating a different name. For example, when starting work on your February newsletter, begin by opening a copy of the "NEWSTEMP" file, but save it under "FEBNEWS."

Style sheets should list the margins, column widths, border thicknesses and other variables that determine the "look" of your publication.

Style Sheets

Use written and stored style sheets to save even more time.

It's important to prepare a written style sheet for each project.

Style sheets can be stored in three-ring binders, next to copies of the finished project. (Over-sized projects can be reduced to binder size by using the reduction feature on photocopiers.)

A back-up copy of your style sheet should be kept at a second location, in the unlikely event the original is lost or damaged. At the end of each chapter, style sheets and checklists are included for each type of document discussed. You may want to copy those pages and use them in your daily work.

Formatting While Writing

Using the formatting abilities built into your word processing program is another time-saver.

That's particularly important when creating projects such as books, in which many blocks of copy are identically formatted throughout the document.

Many word processing programs let you do a lot of formatting as you write the file, before it's used by your desktop publishing program. Further, many word processing programs let you store "electronic style sheets" as separate files, which can be shared and referred to as you prepare different projects.

With a single key, you can define the typeface, type size, leading, style, weight, alignment and other parameters, and assign them to a single sentence or paragraph–or even a complete file. Doing that before the files are placed in your book, brochure or newsletter can save you a lot of time.

Although style sheets usually are associated with word processing, some desktop publishing programs also have them.

Inventory and Planning

Design your desktop publishing projects on the basis of their anticipated content and purpose.

As you read through the chapters that follow—or turn directly to the items of most interest to you—notice how much your projects' designs are influenced by their content and intent.

A newsletter of serious opinion, for example, requires a totally different design than a newsletter featuring lots of pictures and short topics.

A newsletter of serious opinion requires a different design than a newsletter with lots of pictures and short topics.

An image-building magazine ad requires a different design approach than a product- and price-oriented newspaper ad.

The tools of graphic design must be relevant to their function and environment.

Letterhead for a prestigious law firm should look completely different than a letterhead for a rock music promoter.

Appropriateness

The examples in this section bring us full circle to the issue of relevance discussed in Section One.

The tools of graphic design must be relevant to their function and environment. What is appropriate in one situation might be inappropriate in another.

As the samples in this section illustrate, your desktop publishing design skills will grow to the extent that you become sensitive to the correct application of the various graphic tools.

Chapter 8: Newsletters, Catalogs & Tabloids

*Newletters, cata-
logs and tabloids
use timely informa-
tion that requires
frequent updates.*

Newsletters

*The design of most successful newsletters combines several basic
elements.*

Those include masthead, headlines, kickers, teasers, lead-ins,
body copy, jump lines, credits, artwork, captions, publication
information, logo and mailing area.

Size

*Although smaller formats are possible, the standard newsletter is
created by folding an 11" by 17" paper, called a signature, into four
8 1/2" by 11" pages.*

Eight-, twelve- and sixteen-page newsletters are assembled by
using more than one 11" by 17" sheet of paper.

Distribution

The method of distribution should be taken into account when you design your newsletter.

Newsletters can be mailed flat or can be folded in half or triple-folded. In addition, newsletters can be self-mailers or mailed in envelopes.

Decisions about distribution should be made before you proceed with the design of your newsletter. Self-mailers eliminate the cost of envelopes, for example, but sacrifice valuable editorial or selling space used for the mailing area.

A triple-folded newsletter is inexpensive to mail, for example, but the front page and headlines aren't visible until the newsletter is unfolded.

This reduces the "billboard effect" which occurs when an 8 1/2" by 11" newsletter appears in the recipient's mailbox.

Masthead

Your newsletter's masthead provides immediate visual identification and communicates the newsletter's purpose.

A great deal of thought should be devoted to the design of the masthead. Your masthead and logo are the most visible design elements repeated from issue to issue.

Newsletter mastheads usually are placed horizontally at the top of the first page. Mastheads often extend across the full width of the newsletter.

Effective mast-heads can be centered, flush left or flush right.

However, equally effective mastheads can be centered, flush left or flush right.

Although most mastheads are at the top of the newsletter, they also can be placed approximately a third of the way down from the top. That allows a feature headline and article to appear above it.

Although most mastheads are placed horizontally on the page, this masthead is positioned vertically, adding more emphasis to the headline.

Mastheads are positioned vertically sometimes.

A short motto, or explanation, is often placed under the masthead, or is built into the masthead, to amplify its meaning or target the newsletter's intended audience.

Headlines

The number and probable length of stories likely to be included in each issue should influence the design of your newsletter's headlines.

If each issue is likely to focus on a single in-depth article, backed up by several secondary topics, your newsletter design should feature a single, dominant headline.

On the other hand, if your newsletter features several shorter articles, the front page should allow more than one headline to be visible.

Headlines typically are placed above the articles they introduce. However, they also can be placed next to an article.

Headlines can be placed to the side of the copy.

Teasers

Use teasers to invite readers inside your newsletter.

A short table of contents area on the front cover of your newsletter can act as a teaser, drawing attention to articles and features contained inside or on the back cover.

Draw attention to your newsletter's table of contents by placing it in a small, shaded box.

A table of contents on the front cover of your newsletter can act as a teaser.

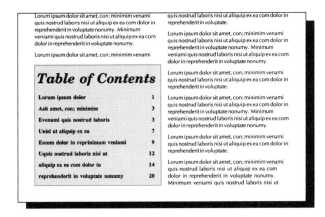

Artwork and Captions

The availability of illustrations and photographs greatly influences your newsletter's design.

If the thrust of your newsletter is factual, and photographs are available, be sure to include space for them. Also include space for captions to accompany each photograph.

On the other hand, if your newsletter emphasizes opinion, and photographs aren't readily available, you can safely devote less emphasis to artwork. In that case, illustrations without captions can be used to strengthen your message.

Publication Information

Readers must be able to easily identify the source of the newsletter.

Be sure to provide space for your organization's logo, as well as your address and phone number.

In most cases, the logo should appear on the front cover and should be large enough to be visible, but not large enough to compete with or overwhelm the masthead.

Your organization's logo can be placed in the masthead.

Readers must be able to identify the source of the newsletter.

Or your logo can be located at the bottom of the front cover. It also can be totally eliminated or only appear on the back cover as long as your organization is identified in some way.

The volume number and date of the newsletter should be prominent.

Lead-ins

Use subheads and short summaries to provide a transition between headlines and body copy.

Lead-ins can be placed between the headline and body copy.

Lead-ins can be placed between the headline and body copy.

Frequently, lead-ins span more than one column.

Alternatively, the lead-in can be placed within the body copy, separated by horizontal rules.

Lead-ins also can take the form of pull-quotes (summaries or direct quotes pulled from an article, frequently placed in a screened box to break up a "gray" page).

Body Copy

Your newsletter design also must take into account the length of the articles likely to be included in each issue.

If your newsletter features long articles, choose a multi-column format, with narrow columns and small type.

The appearance of multi-column newsletters can be improved with thin vertical rules between the columns.

Choose wider columns and larger type, however, if your news-letter emphasizes shorter features.

Credits

If your newsletter is designed to emphasize the credibility of your employees, identify authors by name.

Personalize your newsletter by including a photo or drawing of the author.

If possible, personalize your newsletter by including a photo-graph or drawing of the author.

Mailing Information

If your newsletter is a self-mailer, be sure to provide sufficient space for a mailing label and other mailing information.

The mailing area normally appears at the bottom of the back page.

Be sure to include your firm's or organization's return address next to the mailing label. (Of course, if fulfillment–or mailing list maintenance and addressing–is handled by an outside firm, usually called a lettershop, put that firm's return address in the mailing area.)

Because of their longevity, catalogs often are printed on more expensive paper and include more color.

The mailing area also should clearly indicate whether your newsletter is First- or Third-Class mail. In either case, include your firm's Postal Permit Number to avoid licking stamps.

Adding "Address Correction Requested" above the mailing label area helps you keep your customer or prospect mailing list up-to-date. If you include "Address Correction Requested" in the mailing area of your newsletter, you'll be informed of the new address when a newsletter recipient moves.

Many newsletter mailers choose to include "Address Correction Requested" only once or twice a year.

Catalogs

Catalogs are similar to newsletters, except they usually contain more pages and are more product-oriented.

Catalogs are usually designed for longer shelf life.

Catalogs differ from newsletters in that they're designed for a longer shelf life. Whereas newsletters usually appear bimonthly or quarterly, catalogs frequently are produced on an annual or biannual basis. Because of their longevity, catalogs often are printed on more expensive paper and include more color.

In many cases, particularly in the retail business, catalogs evolve from newsletters.

Covers

Catalog covers often are printed on a different paper stock than the inside pages.

Often, a heavier, glossy (or smooth, reflective) paper stock is used to provide higher quality photo reproduction and better color saturation.

Often, a single photograph of the company's most popular product is used on the cover to communicate the mood of the catalog, as well as sell the featured product.

Alternatively, a collage, or grouping of smaller photographs, can call attention to the diversity of products described inside.

Like newsletters, catalog covers often contain a dominant masthead that describes the contents.

Inside Pages

The inside pages of catalogs often are more heavily formatted than newsletters.

Often, the page format is equally divided into sections for product photographs, captions and prices.

You can add variety by making some photographs or drawings larger than others.

Inside pages of catalogs often are more tightly formatted than newsletters.

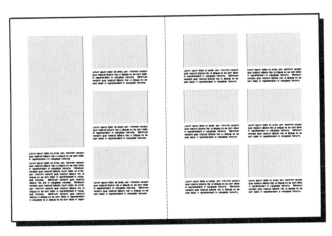

Order Blank

Although ordering information and an order blank can be printed as part of the catalog, response can be increased by providing a separate postage-paid, self-addressed order blank inserted into the middle of the catalog.

That increases sales by making it easy for readers to respond to the catalog's offerings.

The inside front cover usually contains a description of the firm sending the catalog, designed to build customer confidence in the firm's ability to fulfill the order.

Tabloids

Tabloids and newspaper inserts are similar to newsletters, except that their larger page sizes increase design flexibility.

The typical tabloid page is 11" by 17", although those dimensions vary from newspaper to newspaper and printer to printer. Many tabloids are 11" by 14".

Desktop publishing allows last-minute revisions to be easily made, delaying the "final" deadline until the last moment.

Tabloids often are printed on a web press, which means the paper comes off a large roll. As a result, the actual image area of the tabloid is usually smaller than 11" by 17".

Desktop publishing software programs generally allow you to create tabloid pages. Most laser printers, however, are limited to printing on 8 1/2" by 11" sheets of paper.

To get around that limitation, most desktop publishing programs offer an "overlap" feature, which automatically overlaps (or tiles) a series of 8 1/2" by 11" pages that can then be mechanically pasted together to create a large tabloid page.

It's entirely appropriate to use a laser printer to typeset your tabloid because the coarse newsprint used to print most tabloids absorbs ink, reducing the sharpness considered to be a major advantage of phototypesetting. In addition, desktop publishing allows last-minute revisions to be easily made, delaying the "final" deadline until the last possible moment.

Previewing Your Tabloid

You can preview your finished tabloid by printing reduced-size pages.

In order to preview your tabloid before the pages are printed on your laser printer, print them at 65 percent of actual size. That transforms an 11" by 17" tabloid page into an 8 1/2" by 11" size.

As an alternative, you can use the "thumbnail" feature found on most desktop publishing programs to print out an even smaller version of your tabloid. That allows you to print out reduced-size versions of up to 16 pages on a single 8 1/2" by 11" page, making it easy to see your tabloid as a whole and assess how the various pages and spreads fit together.

Front Cover

The front page of a tabloid should contain many of the same elements found on the front page of a newsletter or catalog.

However, the tabloid's larger size allows bolder headlines and larger photographs without sacrificing a large masthead or a significant amount of body copy.

A large photograph can monopolize the tabloid's front cover.

The front page of a tabloid should contain many of the same elements found on the front page of a news-letter or catalog.

Or, the front cover can consist of a large photograph accompanied by a grid of smaller photographs.

In some cases, the front cover consists largely of headline type.

Inside Pages

Choose a consistent format for the inside pages of your tabloid.

Design your tabloid as a series of two-page spreads. Include your organization's logo at least once on every spread. Ideally, each spread should contain the masthead or firm's name, as well as a restatement of the tabloid's title or theme. That information is ideally suited for placement in a deep "sink," or lowered top border, of the tabloid.

Design your tabloid as a series of two-page spreads.

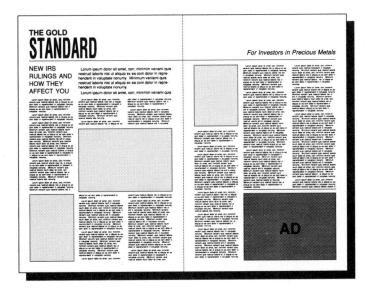

Often, a three-column format is chosen, allowing you to use a variety of photograph sizes.

A five-column format creates additional design flexibility.

A five-column format creates additional design flexibility.

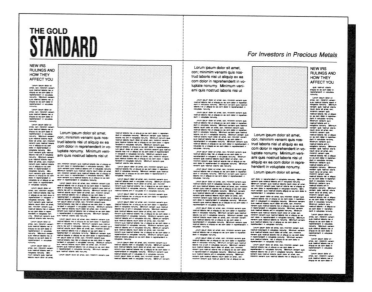

Content

Because of their large size, tabloids allow you to mix editorial and selling space.

You can mix information and advertising in your tabloid in several ways. The mixture can enhance your firm's credibility and image, pre-selling prospective customers on your firm's competence and professionalism. You also can expand the market for your products by answering basic questions first-time buyers might have.

Editorial information can be grouped between parallel rules at the top of each page.

Because of their size, tabloids allow you to mix editorial and selling space.

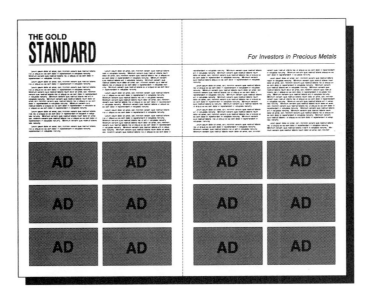

Editorial information can be placed in vertical columns adjacent to the selling area.

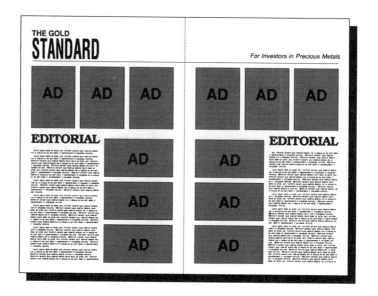

Editorial information can be placed at the bottom of each page.

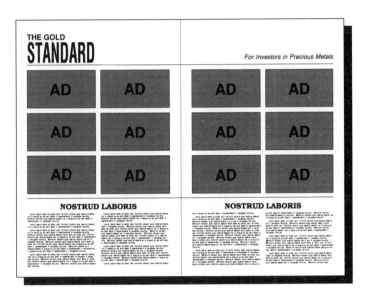

Finally, editorial information can be placed between the selling areas.

A screen behind the editorial material adds to its impact.

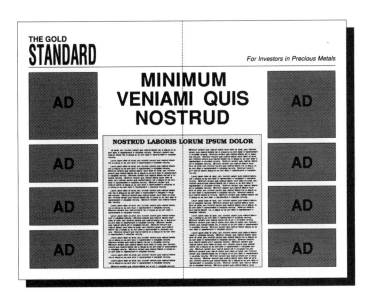

Back Cover

Pay as much attention to the back cover of your tabloid as you do to the front cover.

Many newspaper readers see the back cover before the front. Therefore, you should use the back to summarize important points contained on the front cover.

Other Uses

Newspaper inserts also can be used in-house or as direct mail.

The incremental cost of printing additional newspaper inserts is low. Thus, it often makes sense to print extra copies for use in-house or to mail to past customers–or customers you've targeted as likely prospects.

It's important to remember that newspapers and postal authorities have different requirements. Those may require you to "stop the presses" to make minor adjustments. For example, most newspapers require a printed notice that the tabloid is a "Supplement" to the *Longmount Daily Bugle*. However, that notice cannot be printed on issues sent through the mail independent of the *Longmount Daily Bugle*, or distributed to customers in your store.

Because newspaper readers see the back cover before the front, use the back to summarize important points contained on the front cover.

Checklist for Newsletters, Catalogs and Tabloids

☐ 1. Does your newsletter, catalog or newspaper insert have a distinctive masthead which identifies the subject matter and sets it apart?

☐ 2. Is the masthead amplified by a phrase or motto which further attracts readership?

☐ 3. Are volume number and issue dates clearly identified?

☐ 4. Do headlines compete with the masthead or each other?

☐ 5. Is the source of the publication clearly identified by your logo, supported by address and telephone information?

☐ 6. Are there front-cover "teasers" or a table of contents which direct the reader's interest inside?

☐ 7. Is the design of your newsletter, catalog or newspaper insert appropriate for its content?

☐ 8. Are articles and product categories clearly separated from each other?

☐ 9. Does your catalog contain an order blank to make it easy for readers to respond to your offer?

☐ 10. Have you paid as much attention to the back cover of your publication as the front cover?

☐ 11. Is there a consistency between each issue of your publication, yet enough design variation to attract attention?

☐ 12. Do you monitor your publication and compare it with similar publications sent out by competitors?

Chapter 9: Newspaper & Magazine Ads

Strong borders make a newspaper ad stand apart from the "clutter" surrounding it.

Desktop publishing is ideally suited to producing newspaper advertisements, which tend to have short lead times and frequent content changes. By establishing a series of templates, you can produce newspaper ads quickly and cost-effectively.

Borders

Because most newspaper advertisements occupy less than a full page, pay special attention to borders and white space.

Strong borders make your newspaper ad stand apart from the ads and editorial materials (typically called "clutter") surrounding it. The type of border you choose often will be determined by the shape of the advertisement.

A wide, vertical ad should have strong top and bottom borders .

Thinner side borders make the ad look taller than it actually is.

Thinner side borders make the ad look taller than it actually is.

A smaller, square ad should have borders of equal thickness around all four sides.

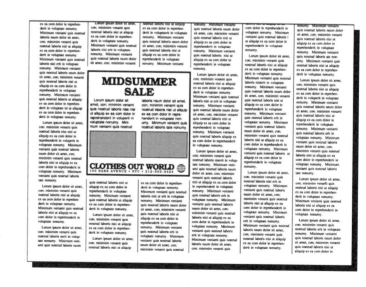

White Space

Use white space to further isolate your newspaper advertisement from its surroundings.

The impact of your ad can be increased by providing sufficient "breathing room" between the borders of the ad and its artwork and copy.

One way to do that is to place the borders of your ad within the space you buy. As a result, there will be white space on both sides of your borders, clearly separating your advertisement from its surroundings.

Use white space to further isolate your newspaper advertisement from its surroundings.

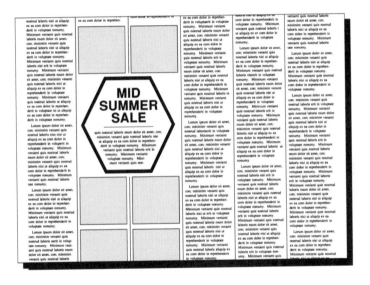

Headlines

Regardless of size, all of your newspaper ads should use the same headline treatment.

One common technique is to reverse the headline out of a box that occupies between a quarter and a third of the space.

Regardless of size, all your newspaper ads should use the same headline treatment.

A shaded background is often used behind the headline and the primary photograph or illustration. That allows the headline to be reversed, yet the body copy can be set in black type against a white background.

Headlines are centered in most newspaper ads, although that doesn't have to be the case.

One very effective technique is to balance a strong flush-right headline with a smaller flush-left subhead. That technique draws readers into the ad more quickly by speeding their transition from "premise" headline to "supporting" subhead.

A flush-right head-line with a smaller flush-left subhead draws readers into the ad more quickly.

Handling Artwork

In multi-product ads, base your layout on the number of products you want to include in your advertisement.

The ad layout you choose should be influenced by the number and size of the products you want to include. The design of your advertisement also should be influenced by the appearance of your competitors' ads.

Pyramid Ad Layouts

Choose a pyramid ad layout when you want to emphasize some products more than others.

A multi-column "pyramid" ad can be extremely effective. It allows for a hierarchical organization. Place a large photograph of your most competitive product at the top of the ad. Immediately below it, place the next two most competitive products. Then, include three or four columns of product listings.

A multi-column "pyramid" ad allows for a hierarchical organization.

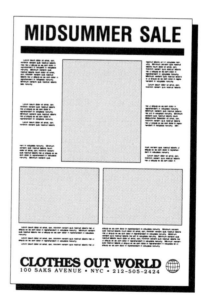

Grid Layouts

When most products are equally important, organize your product offerings in a grid.

As an alternative, photos, captions and prices can be contained within a grid of boxes. Although the basic grid consists of equal-sized boxes, a great deal of flexibility is possible.

Although the basic grid consists of equal-sized boxes, a great deal of flexibility is possible.

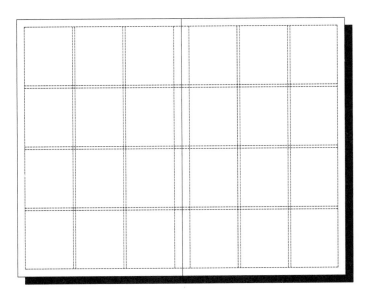

Featured items can be emphasized by placing them in double-wide or double-high boxes.

Featured items can be emphasized by placing them in double-wide or double-high boxes.

Featured items also can be placed in boxes that are four times the size of regular boxes.

Screens can be used behind selected grid boxes to draw attention to featured products.

Column Ads

Choose a column-based ad structure when your competition is using pyramid or grid-based ads.

The products advertised can be organized by category, which is traditionally done by using vertical columns, with subheads at the top of each column identifying the contents.

Products can be organized by category, with subheads at the top of each column identifying the contents.

When two-page spreads are used, however, horizontal columns work just as well. The subheads identifying the contents of each column should be grouped at the left-hand edge of each horizontal column.

Three or four paragraphs of editorial material attract the news-oriented reader.

Breaking Formats for Emphasis

When you've established a format, you can embellish it to suit your particular needs.

For example, in the manner of a tabloid, you can add an "educational" ambience to your ads with call-outs, or brief editorial statements. Those embellishments can balance your "hard-sell" product and price promotions, and sell your store as a desirable destination, as well as selling the particular promotional products you've featured.

Call-outs

Use call-outs to draw attention to the most important selling features of your products.

Call-outs are short rules with arrows on one end that connect product artwork with brief, two- or three-word descriptions of product features and benefits. Call-outs give ads an "educational" feeling. Because the explanations are so brief, the readers get a brief synopsis of why they should buy a particular product.

You can add an "educational" ambience to your ads with call-outs or brief editorial statements.

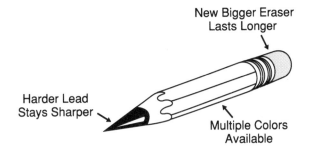

New Bigger Eraser
Lasts Longer

Harder Lead
Stays Sharper

Multiple Colors
Available

Brief Editorial Statements

A few paragraphs of non-selling editorial material can greatly enhance the productivity of the "selling" areas of your ads.

Three or four paragraphs are sufficient to attract the news-oriented reader and position your store as an important resource and reputable place to buy.

Captions, Prices and Logos

The type size used for captions and prices should be proportional to the size of the photograph or artwork used to illustrate the product.

Prices set in large type should accompany large photographs. Prices set in small type should accompany small photographs.

Likewise, manufacturers' logos should be in correct proportion to the size of the ad and surrounding artwork.

In grid-type ads, make all logos the same size and, whenever possible, place them in the same respective position in each box.

Only a few type sizes should be used within an ad.

Practice restraint when choosing typefaces and type sizes. Avoid using a different type size for each product. Only a few type sizes should be used within an ad. Use one type size for "primary" products, and a second size for secondary products.

Not every product advertised must be illustrated. Often, the best-looking ads are those that include only a few representative photographs or drawings.

Logo and Buying Information

Every ad should contain all the information necessary for a customer to make a purchase.

The logo of the firm running the ad should be very prominent, which can be achieved by either size or white space.

In this ad, the logo is relatively small, yet it's easily identified because it's surrounded by white space.

Successful newspaper ads tell a complete story. They make it easy for the reader to respond. Addresses, phone numbers and financing information are clearly visible.

Templates for Newspaper Ads

You can improve your ability to produce newspaper ads by constructing a series of templates for different-sized ads.

Templates speed up production of individual ads by providing a consistent framework for their assembly.

For example, create and save templates for full-page, half-page, third-page and quarter-page ads. Those different sizes of ads should reflect a strong family resemblance, based on a consistent headline and border treatment, plus consistent placement of artwork and buying information.

By preparing templates in advance, you can use them when making product and price decisions. Those templates also will speed up production of individual ads by providing a consistent framework for their assembly.

Including Store Benefits

Although most newspaper ads are product- and price-oriented, store benefits always should be included.

Those benefits can be featured in blocks of space similar to the way "editorial" material and "selling" space are laid out in tabloids.

Alternatively, store benefits can be grouped in a box at the bottom of the ad.

Although most newspaper ads are product-oriented, store benefits always should be included.

Symbols, such as check-marks, can be used to emphasize benefits.

Smaller Newspaper Ads

Desktop publishing is ideally suited to the preparation of one-, two- and three-column newspaper ads.

It's often harder to produce an effective small newspaper ad than a full-page or half-page ad.

Large ads attract attention simply because of their size. Smaller ads have to be designed more carefully, so they'll emerge from the surrounding clutter.

One of the most effective formats for single-column newspaper ads is to reverse the headline out of solid black, focus the ad around a single product and balance the reversed-out headline with a strong logo and address treatment.

Small newspaper ads require a great deal of restraint. It's all too easy to make them complicated and hard to read. Small ads gain impact to the extent that they're focused.

Classified Ads

Desktop publishing can add impact to your "Help Wanted" and other classified ads.

Classified ads are usually prepared by newspapers because most newspapers don't inform advertisers that they can prepare distinctive borders to make their classified ads stand out.

The addition of a prominent border can make a big difference in the response you get to your "Help Wanted" ad.

A prominent border can make a big difference in the response you get to classified advertisements.

venami quis nostrud laboris nisi ut aliquip ex ea com dolor in reprehenderit in voluptate nonumy. Minimum

DESKTOP PUBLISHING

art/production person to help out three tired cowboys and one cowgirl who are working day and night to finish a graphic design book. Must have DTP experience, willing to work long hours, meet hot deadlines and like pizza. Must relocate to Denver Colorado ASAP. Send résumé to Laser Writing Inc. "World Head quarters."

VENIAMI QUIS nostrud laboris erit in voluptate nonumy. Minimum veniami quis nostrud laboris nsum dolor sit amet, con; minimim

NOSTRUD LABORIS nisi ut aliquip ex ea com dolor in reprehenderit in voluptate nonumy. Minimum veniami quis nostrud Laboris erit in voluptate nonumy. Minimum veniami quis nostrud laboris nsum dolor sit amet, con; minimim veniami quis nostrud

171

Quality Considerations

It's entirely appropriate to prepare camera-ready newspaper ads using your laser printer.

It's usually not necessary to go to the expense of phototype-setting your newspaper ads, because the relatively coarse newsprint absorbs the ink to such a degree that the quality advantage offered by phototypesetting is lost.

Another advantage of using desktop publishing is that many retail ads use line-art instead of photographs. That means you can use a scanner to build a database of frequently used illustrations, which then can be placed in your ad and scaled to size.

In addition, scanners and desktop publishing programs are rapidly improving in their ability to handle photographs. The quality produced on a laser printer soon will approach the quality of newspaper photo reproduction. Thus, it's entirely feasible that you soon will be able to prepare complete newspaper ads, including photographs, on your desktop publishing system and laser printer.

Magazine Advertisements

Magazine advertisements generally feature fewer products and require higher levels of production quality.

Fewer products are included, because of the long lead time between when the ad is placed and when it appears in print.

Magazine ads generally appear in a more dignified atmosphere. Fewer size options are available. Most magazines are created around a three-column grid.

That limits available advertising options to full-page, half-page horizontal, half-page vertical, two-thirds or one-third page vertical, two-thirds or one-third page horizontal and one-sixth page vertical or horizontal (see next page). You should prepare basic formats (or grids, including borders, logo placement) for the two or three size alternatives you're likely to use. Those will speed up the planning and production of your ads.

Because most magazines are printed on high-quality, coated paper, advertisements created with desktop publishing should be produced on a phototypesetter. Laser printing often doesn't provide the sharpness necessary for the best possible presentation of your ad.

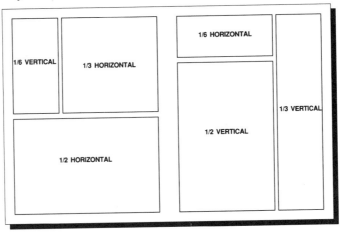

Borders, headlines and white space are crucial elements of successful magazine advertisements.

Your ad must appear as a self-contained unit, separated from surrounding editorial material and other advertisements. The relatively small size of most magazine ads presents a major challenge. Readers typically will see your ad as part of a horizontal 11" by 17" spread. In addition, you generally don't know where your ad will appear in the magazine.

Magazine advertisements generally feature fewer products and require higher levels of production quality.

Another difficulty is that your ad may be dwarfed by surrounding color ads.

Magazine ads often include coupons inviting prospective customers to send for further information. Because those coupons should be placed at the lower right-hand corner of the ad, request lower right-hand page placement when running an ad that includes a coupon.

With most desktop publishing programs, you can create distinctive borders for your coupons.

A great deal of attention should be devoted to the design of the coupon. Once created, however, it can be stored as a separate file and used over and over again.

Avoid Unusable Coupons

Avoid creating coupons and forms with lines spaced so closely together a customer would have difficulty completing them.

Always make it as easy as possible for readers to respond to your offer or complete your form.

Name and address areas also should be long enough to be legibly completed.

Line spacing on forms designed to be filled out with a typewriter should conform to normal typewriter spacing.

Color

Magazine ads frequently include color.

Color can be used as background, or spot color can be used to highlight headlines or organizers such as rules and borders. Or, color can be restricted to photography.

The newer desktop publishing programs allow you to make spot-color separations that you can give your printer. When used in combination with heat-sensitive, color-sensitive transfers, color separations can be used to quickly create color layouts of your project.

Checklist for Newspaper and Magazine Advertisements

☐ 1. Is your ad set off from its surroundings by appropriate margins, borders and white space?

☐ 2. Is the headline large enough to attract attention without overwhelming other elements of the ad?

☐ 3. Are captions and prices clearly related to product photographs or illustrations?

☐ 4. Has all important buying information—address, hours, credit terms—been clearly spelled out?

☐ 5. Is your firm's logo prominent enough to provide a visual signature for your ad?

☐ 6. Is the design of your ad appropriate to both its content (the number and importance of products included) and the image you want to project?

☐ 7. Is the design of your ad consistent with other advertisements you've produced?

☐ 8. Is the appearance of your ad clearly different from ads run by your competitors?

Chapter 10: Brochures, Books & Training Materials

Unlike newsletters, brochures are designed for a longer shelf life.

Brochures, books and technical training manuals present design challenges similar to those of advertisements. The biggest challenges are creating readers' interest in your publication and helping them locate information quickly. Another challenge is to make each page–or two-page spread–different from the ones that precede or follow it, without disturbing the publication's overall design integrity.

Brochures

Unlike newsletters, tabloids and advertisements, brochures are designed for a longer shelf life.

Thus, more care should go into designing and producing them.

Because brochures address a more targeted audience, their front covers often present a more dignified, "soft sell" approach. Thus, many front covers contain few words...the minimum necessary to draw the reader inside.

Formats

Choose the format and size which best suit the purpose of your brochure.

Often, the brochure's format is determined by its method of distribution. If it's going to be mailed, for example, it should be designed to fit inside a number ten business envelope.

One of the most common brochure formats is an 8 1/2" by 11" piece of paper folded to create six vertical panels, each approximately 3 1/4" wide by 8 1/2" high.

The brochure's format is determined by its method of distribution.

inside
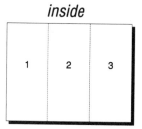

outside
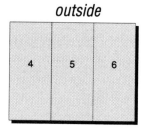

Although the vertical format is most common, the same format can be printed horizontally.

The next step up is an eight-panel brochure printed on a slightly larger sheet of paper. Again, the brochure can be printed horizontally or vertically.

inside
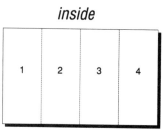

outside
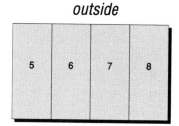

Production Options

You can create six-panel brochures as a series of individual panels or as two sets of side-by-side panels.

The advantage of creating a six-panel brochure as a series of individual pages is that it's unlikely you'll make a mistake in laying out the pages. The disadvantage is that the elements of each panel must be lined up with the panels surrounding it.

When a six-panel brochure is created on two 8 1/2" by 11" pages, remember to correctly organize the sequence of pages. Also remember that the front and back covers are adjacent, yet the third panel actually faces the inside spread.

Another disadvantage of creating brochures as a series of panels on a few sheets of paper is that the image area of most laser printers doesn't cover a full 8 1/2" by 11" sheet of paper. That means you won't be able to bleed color off the edges of each panel unless you output your brochure on a phototypesetter.

Most desktop publishing software programs can print crop marks that make it easy for your commercial printer to accurately line up each page.

Larger Formats

Choose large-format, four-panel and six-panel brochures for point-of-sale use.

Each panel can be as large as 8 1/2" by 11". Actual image area will be smaller, in most cases, because of the limitations of most laser printers. Those brochures must be mailed in larger envelopes at extra cost.

Large point-of-sale brochures are required if they'll be displayed in literature racks.

Over-size brochures also are appropriate if they're to be used primarily as point-of-sale handouts.

Regardless of size, most brochures are similar in layout.

Most desktop publishing software programs can print crop marks that make it easy for commercial printers to accurately line up each page.

Although they offer endless diversity, brochures usually are based on a consistent treatment of the basic design elements.

Covers

Cover design should be based on distribution.

If the brochure is to be displayed in a literature rack, the headline and other identifying information should be placed near the top of the front cover.

Often, the cover consists of a photograph and a large headline.

Although they offer endless diversity, brochures usually are based on a consistent treatment of the basic design elements.

Sometimes, it consists of a series of small photographs instead of a large one.

Often, there are no photographs at all. Instead, the headline is the dominant visual element.

Frequently, a subhead is used to amplify the brochure's headline and lure readers inside.

Frequently, a subhead is used to amplify the brochure's headline and lure readers inside.

Inside Pages

A brochure should be organized for easy left-to-right reading.

One of the best ways to do that is to organize body copy and photographs around a strong horizontal line that continues from page to page.

Use a continuous horizontal line to create uniformity.

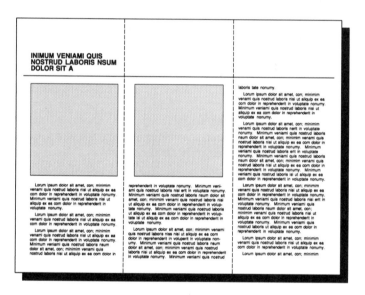

Six-panel brochures offer the advantage of an additional dominant photograph area that can be used to balance the body copy contained inside.

The sixth panel also can be used to summarize information presented in greater detail on the inside pages. Or, it can introduce a new topic.

Back Pages

The back page of a brochure typically contains details and specifications.

The back panel also frequently contains buying information, such as addresses, warranty terms and ordering information.

The method of distribution affects a brochure's design.

Once again, the method of distribution affects design. If the brochure is a self-mailer, you must include space for an address label and postage.

If the brochure is to be used at the point of sale, be sure to leave space for dealers or distributors to stamp their names and addresses.

An interesting six-panel effect can be easily created by adding an extra fold to a single sheet of 11" by 17" paper.

By simply folding in the left-hand panel, it's possible to add variety to a simple four-panel brochure.

Fold-in flaps are useful for quotations and testimonials.

The additional fold creates two additional viewing areas. Although the front panel becomes slightly narrower, it's offset by a vertical block that's visible both when the brochure is closed, and when it's open.

The fold-in flap also creates another discrete viewing area. That narrow panel is useful for quotations and testimonials.

Type and Artwork

Typography, white space and artwork are a brochure's most important design elements.

Because a brochure typically is viewed by itself, borders aren't as important as they are in advertisements.

The type treatment of headlines, subheads and body copy becomes more important, however. Careful attention to typography pays off by enhancing a brochure's selling power.

Careful attention to typography enhances a brochure's selling power.

Books

More and more books are being submitted to publishers in camera-ready form.

Desktop publishing gives authors control of the appearance as well as the content of their books.

Desktop publishing offers another advantage. Because it reduces the time and cost of production, publishers can afford to take chances on books that otherwise might not be printed.

Book design involves a different set of priorities than the design of newsletters, advertisements or brochures. For instance, page-to-page consistency and visual organization are more important for books than for brochures.

Desktop publishing allows publishers to take chances on books that otherwise might not be printed.

A great deal of planning is necessary if text and artwork are to be properly balanced with a continuing structure.

Art Considerations

Artwork plays an important role in book design.

A book with numerous illustrations and photographs requires a different layout than a text-oriented book.

A book describing the evolution of a painter's style requires a different layout than a novel or economics textbook.

Style Considerations

Fiction and nonfiction require different page structures.

Likewise, book design should take into account the writer's style.

If the author frequently uses long paragraphs, a single wide column is appropriate.

If, however, the author's style is based on shorter paragraphs, a two-column format might be more appropriate.

The author's use of subheads also must be taken into account. Fiction and nonfiction require different page structures.

Nonfiction books frequently use subheads to introduce new topics. Those subheads are often set off in a narrow column.

Because they rarely use subheads, fiction books are easier to design. A single wide column often suffices.

Organizing Elements

Attention must be paid to planning and organizing a book.

Readers must be kept constantly informed. They must be able to see at a glance which chapter they're reading and quickly locate information by checking the headers.

In addition, each new chapter should be introduced in a distinctive way. Properly handled, those chapter introductions lure a person to read on.

Each chapter should be introduced in a way that lures a person to read on.

*Training materials
often are more
sectioned
than books.*

Often, different formats are used for different sections of a book. The information at the front of the book–the introduction, table of contents, etc.–is often organized around a different page layout than that used for the book itself. Back matter–index, bibliography and appendices–requires yet another format.

Book design must accommodate those different demands without sacrificing the book's overall coherence or unity.

Training Manuals

Training manuals and software documentation present even stronger organizational challenges.

Whereas most books are read from cover to cover, many readers of training manuals or software documentation want to go directly to the pages that answer their questions.

Thus, training materials often are more sectioned than books. The topics covered on each page (or spread) must be emphasized. In that way, training manuals are more similar to dictionaries or encyclopedias than books.

Production Considerations

Desktop publishing is ideal for producing books and training manuals.

Because so many variables remain the same from page to page, books and associated publications (e.g., training manuals or software documentation) are projects in which electronic stylesheets can be extremely valuable. If you're involved in producing many of them, you'll want to pay particular attention to the formatting and style sheet capabilities of the word processing and desktop publishing software programs you choose.

Word processing and desktop publishing software programs differ in their ability to organize and format books. Some programs automatically prepare a detailed index, table of contents and list of illustrations!

Checklist for Brochures, Books and Manuals

Brochures

☐ 1. Is the design and format of your brochure appropriate for its method of distribution?

☐ 2. Does the front cover of your brochure or book contain a headline or copy which invites the reader to read on?

☐ 3. Are details and specifications included on the back page to summarize important points?

☐ 4. Is there a smooth and logical development of ideas from the front to back covers?

Books and Manuals

☐ 1. Does the book's design reflect the author's writing style and the number and type of illustrations or photographs?

☐ 2. Is the book or manual organized to make information easy to find?

☐ 3. Are illustrations set off by sufficient white space?

☐ 4. Do two-page spreads present an orderly appearance when viewed together?

Chapter 11: Business Correspondence

Business corre-spondence must communicate obvious and sub-conscious informa-tion at a glance.

As you develop your design sense and become more familiar with the capabilities of your desktop publishing system, you'll continue to discover new applications. You'll probably find that in-house projects can be produced more quickly with desktop publishing than when design, typesetting and layout had to be farmed out to independent contractors.

Letterheads

Letterheads can be surprisingly complicated.

That's because letterheads often must communicate a lot of obvious and subconscious information at a glance.

The information on a letterhead must be complete. Yet, the letter-head must not detract from the message it's communicating. In addition, there should be space for creating an ambience, or environment, which reflects the tone of the company. Obviously, a lawyer's letterhead should have a totally different appearance than a rock music promoter's letterhead (see Chapter 9).

The elements of a successful letterhead include

- Business name
- Logo
- Motto or business philosophy
- Street address and mailing address (if different)
- Phone number
- Telex or facsimile number

In addition, corporate and nonprofit letterheads often list officers or board members.

All too often, that leaves little space for the actual message area of the letter!

The most typical problem is a logo that is so large it visually overwhelms the letterhead.

The most typical problem is a logo that is so large it visually overwhelms the letterhead.

U.S. TRANSPORTATION

183 Main St • Hotchkiss, CO 80367 • (303) 532-6324

A second problem concerns omitted information. Letterhead design becomes complicated when it must include both telephone and facsimile numbers, or separate street addresses and post office box numbers (often with different Zip Codes).

One common mistake is to print a telephone number without the area code. That's all right for local callers, but puts long-distance callers at a distinct disadvantage!

The final difficulty in organizing letterheads involves separating the body copy of a letter from the letterhead itself. However, that problem can be resolved in one of several ways.

Sometimes, the "live area" of the letterhead is boxed.

Another difficulty in designing letterhead involves defining the space for body copy.

Other times, a horizontal rule is used to set off the message area. A single vertical rule serves the same function.

The letterhead design should be carried over to the envelope design.

The design of the letterhead should be carried over to the envelope design.

More and more business communications are designed for "window" envelopes, eliminating the need for typing separate envelopes or address labels. The design of the letterhead must allow the recipient's address to be visible through the window.

Business Cards

Many of the problems encountered in letterhead design also occur in designing business cards.

That's because a lot of information must be presented in a relatively small space (usually just 3 1/2" by 2"). Not only must addresses, phone numbers and a logo be included, but the individual's name and position must be prominently displayed.

Business cards are an ideal application of desktop publishing technology.

Business cards are an ideal application of desktop publishing technology. When the basic card has been designed and stored as a template, it takes a few seconds to replace one individual's name and position with another name and position.

Those revisions can be done when the person is present, eliminating chances for misspelled names or incorrect job titles.

Price Sheets, Statements and Quote Forms

Desktop publishing makes it easy to prepare price sheets, policy statements and quote forms.

Written communications receive more respect than verbal communications. Their tangibility discourages bickering and arguments and eliminates ambiguity.

Because prices can be quickly updated, desktop publishing is ideally suited to preparing price sheets and policy statements.

Many retailers or self-employed professionals combine price sheets with quote sheets, making it easy for prospective buyers to "sell themselves."

Press Releases

Desktop publishing makes it easy to prepare effective press releases.

Newspaper and magazine editors each week get hundreds of press releases, most of which receive a quick glance before being consigned to the circular file (i.e., wastebasket).

Well-designed press releases can help your message emerge from the clutter.

A well-designed press release provides the editor with all the information he or she needs to decide whether to read on. That includes the topic of the press release, as well as sources for further information.

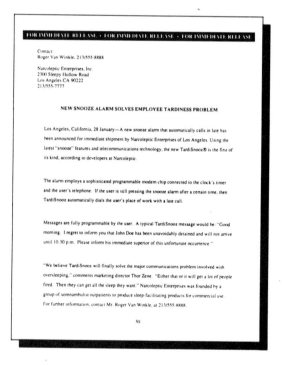

Subheads within the body of the press release help editors to quickly grasp the important points. In skimming the subheads, editors are more likely to read the full release.

Desktop publishing's ability to help you orchestrate a hierarchy of information can help your press releases receive the attention they deserve.

Checklists for Business Correspondence

Letterheads and Envelopes

☐ 1. Does the design of your letterhead, envelopes and business cards accurately reflect your firm's philosophy and business?

☐ 2. Is your firm's logo, with address/phone number, in correct proportion to the message area of your letterhead?

☐ 3. Is the message area of your letterhead clearly set apart from background information?

☐ 4. Is all important information included, such as separate mailing and street addresses, facsimile numbers and telephone numbers (including area code)?

☐ 5. Do envelopes repeat important information—including telephone and FAX numbers? (Often, envelopes become separated from letters.)

☐ 6. Do your business cards contain all necessary information as well as the individual's name and position?

Press Releases

☐ 1. Do your press releases present a "newsworthy" feeling?

☐ 2. Do your press releases make it easy for editors to request further information?

Chapter 12: Increasing Your Productivity

*Learning the
ins and outs
of a developing
technology can
be frustrating, but
the alternative is
to be left behind.*

A serious commitment to desktop publishing can increase your efficiency and profitability in the years to come. For example, by going through the process of designing your firm's logo with desktop publishing (or adapting it to your system), you can use your work over and over again.

By saving your logo, business name, address and phone number as separate draw-type files, you can easily use them in both large and small projects–and they'll always look good.

The same files can be scaled down for use on a letterhead, increased in size for a brochure, and made even larger for newspaper ads and tabloids.

The cost of scanning a logo and optimizing it for desktop publishing manipulation will be more than offset as you use the logo again and again.

Learning the ins and outs of a developing technology can be frustrating at times...but the alternative is to be left farther and farther behind.

Desktop publishing capabilities are increasing by leaps and bounds. Yesterday's "impossibilities" are today's realities. Prices are dropping as more and more individuals and corporations discover the advantages of designing and producing their own advertisements and publications. As consumers enter the market, prices will continue to drop.

Creative Experimentation

Consider the 20/80 rule–mastering 20 percent of the basic tools of graphic design will reward you with an 80 percent success rate in your desktop publishing efforts.

So, how do you move from 80 percent to 100 percent?

The answer is time.

Your desktop publishing design capabilities will improve to the extent that you become "creatively dissatisfied" with your efforts–and continue to experiment to find new solutions.

Your design capabilities will improve as you continue working on a project, striving to improve it, even after you've completed it and sent it to the printer!

Sincere Imitation

Your design skills and abilities will improve to the extent that you press your hardware and software capabilities to the limits–analyzing the work of others and trying to uncover the process which led to their particular design solution.

For example, you might try to reproduce award-winning advertisements and brochures on the screen of your computer. Take an issue of *The New Yorker*, for example, and try to reproduce a page that includes both editorial and advertisements.

With desktop publishing, yesterday's impossibilities are today's realities.

Or, go to the library and borrow *The One Show*, or the December issue of *Communication Arts*, which highlight the world's most beautiful advertisements. Try to recreate those ads on your computer. The point isn't to imitate ads that cost tens of thousands of dollars to produce, but to go through the process of putting together such successful ads and carefully examining their design elements.

Imaginary Advertisements

Try creating advertisements for imaginary products.

After you've finished producing your first project with your new desktop publishing system, spend an hour a day creating advertisements for imaginary products.

Software documentation often contains dozens of design tips and tricks.

You might want to enroll in an evening college course or a two-day workshop, and use that as a jumping-off place for creative adventuring.

Return to Basics

Refer to the documentation that came with your software program.

All too often, program documentation is put aside after the basics of the program are mastered. As a result, users don't learn the dozens of tips often featured in the documentation.

Rereading the documentation, or repeating the self-paced tutorial, can free you from unnecessary obstacles, as well as provide added insight into how your desktop publishing hardware and software perform. In addition, it can spark your interest in exploring the limits of your system's capabilities.

As you approach those limits, you'll also approach the limits of your creativity. And you'll probably begin to violate many of the rules outlined in this book. That's good! Truly creative design often involves a balance between the rules and the exceptions.

As you relax and become more comfortable with your program, your capabilities will increase geometrically, and you'll acquire design skills you never thought possible.

Appendix: Writing for Better Design

Desktop Publishing's Strength Is Also Its Achilles' Heel

By offering the flexibility to quickly and easily vary type size, column width and letter, word and line spacing, desktop publishing often can lull you into a false sense of security.

Copywriting and copyfitting used to be considered an intrinsic part of the design process, forcing you to write copy to fit the available space. However, the flexibility built into desktop publishing systems often encourages last-minute text manipulations that can undermine the publication's design integrity.

Good-looking publications result from consistency. Type size and letter, word and line spacing should remain consistent from page to page and article to article. Change should only take place when mandated by design considerations.

Desktop publishing's power makes last-minute changes easy. Avoid the temptation to increase type size and line spacing when an article isn't long enough to fit the space allotted to it. Also avoid the temptation to reduce type size, leading and tracking when you have more than can comfortably fit into available space.

Which Comes First—the Chicken or the Egg?

The issue of copyfitting is a fundamental one.

Beginning desktop publishers tend to design a format for a publication, then "shoehorn" previously written text into it. This problem is compounded when multiple contributors are involved in a publication. Each contributor writes an article of arbitrary length, determined solely by the number of words that the author feels is necessary "to say what needs to be said." The word processed file is then given to someone else for editing and placement in the publication.

This "backwards" approach can destroy consistency and, with it, the publication's appearance. It also wastes time and weakens the publication's content because by the time the editor (or desktop publisher) receives the copy, there often isn't time to do the careful editing which would strengthen the article and seamlessly integrate it into the publication.

As a result, the desktop publisher is tempted to take the easy way out and reduce or enlarge type size, line spacing, letter and word spacing or column width. Or the desktop publisher arbitrarily cuts or "pads" the article to fit available space—again, weakening the article's message.

Copyfitting Offers a Better Alternative

Write your documents to fit available space.

Writing to fit available space—or copyfitting—strengthens both the content and appearance of a document, forcing you to "say what has to be said" in the right amount of space.

Copyfitting involves a three-step process:

1) Decide how much space will be devoted to each feature. Create "thumbnails," or reduced-sized layouts of each page of your document. The amount of space to be allotted to each feature should be based on its relevance to the goals of the publication (see previous chapters).

2) Quantify the space available for each feature before writing copy. This space can be quantified in terms of characters, words or column inches of text.

Each word processing program offers its own way of quantifying copy length. Contributors must keep an eye on document length as they write their articles, and self-edit their copy until their article or feature says what has to be said in the right amount of space.

3) Make final edits only to eliminate widows and orphans and clean up glaring errors.

An Easy Approach to Copyfitting

One of the easiest approaches to copyfitting involves setting the margins on the screen of your word processor to equal the number of words which will fit on a typeset column.

For example, assume that your completed desktop published publication will be set in 10-point Times Roman type set in columns 18 picas wide.

First, using your desktop publishing program, set up a 18-pica column and type out a typical line of text set in 10-point Times Roman type.

The quick brown fox jumps over the lazy dog. The

Next, count the number of characters that fit on the line. Notice that the typical line includes 49 characters.

Then, set the margins on your word processor to equal the number of characters on your typeset line. In this case, you might find that your margins would be 2 1/4 and 2 1/4 inches.

```
The quick brown fox jumps over the lazy dog.  The
```

Although this method won't be 100 percent accurate (depending on word breaks and alignment), you now have roughly a one-to-one relationship between a line of word processed copy and a line of typeset copy.

Finally, determine how many lines of word processed copy are needed to fill the space available for the article or feature. Simply count the number of lines per column inch set in the type size and leading you've chosen. Let's assume you're setting 10-point type on 11-point leading.

The quick brown fox jumps over the lazy dog. The quick brown fox jumps over the lazy dog. The quick brown fox jumps over the lazy dog. The quick brown fox jumps over the lazy dog.The quick brown fox jumps over the lazy dog. The quick brown fox jumps over the lazy dog. The quick brown fox jumps over the lazy dog. The quick brown fox jumps over the lazy dog. The quick brown fox jumps over the lazy dog. The quick brown fox jumps over the lazy dog. The quick brown fox jumps over the lazy dog.

As the above example shows, each column inch contains 8 lines of typeset copy when 10-point Times Roman type is set on 11-point leading.

By simply multiplying the lines per inch by the number of column inches devoted to each article or feature, you can obtain approximate line count for your document.

This is the simplest formula, one which will work with all word processing software programs. When using this formula, word processed copy should be prepared single-spaced, to aid in line counting (even though word processed copy is usually printed double-spaced for ease in editing).

Alternative Approaches to Copyfitting

There are, of course, other approaches to copyfitting.

These involve specifying article length in terms of word counts or character counts. The alternative you choose should be based on the way your word processing program keeps track of article length. Some programs count characters, others count words. These functions are usually accessed through the word processing program's spell-check feature, although some word processing programs inform you of document length each time you save a file.

In all cases, the basic principle is the same. The goal is to relate desired article length in terms of word processed characters or words to the length of the desktop published article in terms of typeset characters or words.

The Specific Method Isn't Important

What is important, however, is that copywriting and copyfitting be viewed as an essential part of the design process. The length of the articles you write or assign should be related to the amount of space they will occupy in the finished publication. Otherwise, you'll end up hurting document integrity and the strength of your articles by forcing last-minute changes in type size, leading or word spacing, or weakening the article by last-minute editing.

Bibliography and Sources

Books

Adobe Systems, Inc., **PostScript Language Tutorial and Cookbook**, Addison-Wesley Publishing, Reading, MA, 1986.

Desktop publishing is based on the PostScript programming language. This book, and the one which follows, are essential to any desktop publisher seeking an advanced understanding of PostScript and the hardware and software which use it.

Adobe Systems, Inc., **PostScript Language Reference Manual**, Addison-Wesley Publishing, Reading, MA, 1986.

A companion volume, organized for easy access.

Adobe Systems, Inc., **The Adobe Type Catalog**, Adobe Systems, Inc., Palo Alto, CA, 1987.

When you want to move beyond the typefaces built into your laser printer, **The Adobe Type Catalog** shows which typefaces are available as downloadable fonts. Each typeface is illustrated, along with suggested applications.

Beach, Mark, **Editing Your Newsletter: A Guide to Writing, Design and Production**, Coast to Coast Books, Portland, OR, 1982.

A simple, straightforward introduction to the field, written during pre-desktop publishing days. Contains numerous sample layouts.

Bly, Robert W., **The Copywriter's Handbook: A Step-By-Step Guide To Writing Copy That Sells**, Dodd, Mead & Company, New York, NY, 1986.

Effective publication design begins with choosing the right words and organizing them in a logical fashion. **The Copywriter's Handbook** helps you do that—even if you're preparing your first advertisement, brochure, newsletter or press release. **The Copywriter's Handbook** updates and expands upon the "classic" rules of copywriting of an earlier generation of advertising professionals, like David Ogilvy and John Caples.

Bly, Robert W., **Create the Perfect Sales Piece: A Do-It-Yourself Guide to Producing Brochures, Catalogs, Flyers, and Pamphlets**, John Wiley & Sons, New York, NY, 1987.

Written for entrepreneurs and executives with new responsibilities, **Create the Perfect Sales Piece** guides readers through the process of planning, copywriting and designing an effective print communication. The book places a great deal of emphasis on advance planning and scheduling.

Brigham, Nancy, **How To Do Leaflets, Newsletters and Newspapers**, Hastings House, New York, NY, 1982.

Written in pre-desktop publishing days, **How To Do Leaflets, Newsletters and Newspapers** remains a useful introduction to the correct use of the various formats.

Caples, John, **Tested Advertising Methods**, Prentice-Hall, Englewood, NJ, 1978.

Tested Advertising Methods offers classic, no-nonsense advice. It helps you "write for results" and shows how to choose the right copy appeal. Separate chapters are devoted to headlines, initial paragraphs and testing your ads. Chapter 15, "What Kinds of Layouts and Illustrations Attract the Most Readers?" will be of special interest to desktop publishers.

Craig, James, **Designing with Type**, Watson-Guptil, New York, NY, 1980.

A comprehensive coverage of the characteristics of the various typefaces and how they can be best employed. Contains special sections devoted to display type, body copy and copyfitting.

Danuloff, Craig and McClelland, Deke, **The Typefaces Of Desktop Publishing,** Publishing Resources, Boulder, CO, 1987.

The Typefaces of Desktop Publishing is a catalog illustrating virtually every Postscript font available for Apple Macintosh computers. A full alphabet of each typeface is shown, including bold and italic variations. **The Typefaces of Desktop Publishing** includes useful hints, technical data and vendor/pricing information.

Felici, James and Nace, Ted, **Desktop Publishing Skills: A Primer For Typesetting with Computers and Laser Printers**, Addison-Wesley, Reading, MA, 1987.

An excellent and highly readable introduction to the subject, which begins by describing the various steps involved in traditional publishing and compares them to electronic publishing methods. Chapter 8, "The Machinery of Desktop Publishing," compares the Apple Macintosh to MS-DOS alternatives.

Hudson, Howard Penn, **Publishing Newsletters: A Complete Guide to Markets, Editorial Content, Design, Printing, Subscriptions, Management, and Much More...,** Charles Scribner's Sons, New York, NY, 1982.

A standard in the field, **Publishing Newsletters** is written by the publisher of the popular "Newsletter on Newsletters." Contains numerous layout ideas and an extensive bibliography and glossary.

Hurlburt, Allen, **Publication Design: A Guide to Page Layout, Typography, Format and Style**, Van Nostrand Reinhold, New York, NY, 1971.

Written for graphics professionals, **Publication Design** discusses the underlying issues behind the design of major magazines.

Hurlburt, Alan, **The Grid**, Van Nostrand Reinhold, New York, NY, 1978.

Illustrates how grids can be used in developing page layouts for newspapers, magazines and books.

Kleper, Michael L., **The Illustrated Handbook of Desktop Publishing and Typesetting**, Tab Books, Blue Ridge Summit, PA, 1987.

This book is the best introduction to the wide range of hardware and software options available for both MS-DOS and Apple Macintosh computers. Contains more than 700 pages of information.

Middleton, Tony, **A Desktop Publisher's Guide To Pasteup: A Do-It-Yourself Guide to Preparing Camera-Ready Pasteups and Mechanicals**, Plusware, Colorado Springs, CO, 1987.

A Desktop Publisher's Guide To Pasteup provides a practical answer to the question, "What do you do with the pages which come out of your laser printer?" It describes the tools needed to prepare pasteups and how to use them. **A Desktop Publisher's Guide to Pasteup** also explains how to choose the right commercial printers to duplicate your job and how to deal with them.

Nelson, Roy Paul, **The Design of Advertising**, Wm. C. Brown Company, Dubuque, IA.

A classic college text, **The Design of Advertising** succeeds because of its numerous examples and "hands-on" conversational style. Fourteen of its 16 chapters are devoted to print advertising.

Nelson, Roy Paul, **Publication Design**, Wm. C. Brown Company, Dubuque, IA, 1984.

This companion volume concentrates on magazine, newspaper and newsletter design, although Chapter 11, "Miscellaneous Publications," also describes brochures and direct mail.

Makuta, Daniel J. and Lawrence, William F., **The Complete Desktop Publisher**, "Compute!" Publications, Greensboro, NC, 1986.

An informed overview of the field, this book places emphasis on function rather than specific hardware or software.

New York Art Directors Club, **The One Show**, Watson-Guptil Publications, New York, NY.

The One Show is a one-stop source for viewing the nation's finest advertising. Each year, the nation's leading art directors submit their best work to a jury of their peers. **The One Show** includes the entries in each category and showcases the winners. Because of its inspirational value, this book is an important addition to your collection.

Ogilvy, David, **Confessions of an Advertising Man,** Atheneum, New York, NY, 1980.

A perennial best-seller, **Confessions of an Advertising Man** is as valuable today as it was when it first appeared almost 20 years ago. It provides desktop publishers with a new perspective on their readers' needs. **Confessions of an Advertising Man** replaces "exploitive" philosophies with a deep underlying respect for the reader's intelligence and basic need for information.

Pantone, Inc., **Pantone Color Selector,** Pantone, Inc., Moonachie, NJ.

Searching for specific colors to set your publication apart from the conventional? The **Pantone Color Selector** contains all ink colors numbered and displayed on both coated and uncoated paper stock. You can easily choose the colors which work best, by themselves or in combination with each other.

Pickens, Judy E., **The Copy-to-Press Handbook: Preparing Words and Art for Print**, John Wiley & Sons, New York, NY, 1985.

Although written in pre-desktop-publishing days, **The Copy-to-Press Handbook** provides a good perspective on book and brochure publishing by combining an overview of traditional methods of phototypesetting and pasteup with a detailed examination of the printing process.

Rinearson, Peter and Woodcock, JoAnne, **Microsoft Word Style Sheets,** Microsoft Press, Redmond, WA, 1987.

Although written specifically for Microsoft Word users, the basic concepts involved in formatting a document during the word processing phase can be helpful to users of other desktop publishing programs.

Seybold, John and Dressler, Fritz, **Publishing from the Desktop,** Bantam Books, New York, NY, 1987.

A technical overview of the various aspects of typography and typesetting, with an emphasis on how the various imaging systems differ. Separate chapters cover image scanners and modifying line art and halftones.

Stone, Robert, **Successful Direct-Marketing Methods**, Crain Books, Chicago, IL, 1982.

Recommended for any desktop publisher who develops direct mail brochures, this book covers all aspects of planning and producing effective direct mail.

University of Chicago, **A Manual of Style**, 13th ed., The University of Chicago Press, Chicago, IL, 1982.

A Manual of Style should be kept next to your computer. Its tightly packed 700-plus pages provide the answers to questions asked by the most conscientious editor, publisher or copywriter. It describes the proper way to handle punctuation, illustrations, quotations, abbreviations, as well as design and typography.

Webb, Robert A., ed. **The Washington Post Deskbook On Style,** McGraw-Hill, New York, NY, 1978.

The Washington Post Deskbook On Style provides precise and quick answers to commonly encountered questions concerning abbreviation, capitalizations, numerals, punctuation and spelling.

White, Alex, **How to Spec Type,** Watson-Guptil, New York, NY, 1987.

How to Spec Type is a very readable, tightly organized introduction to all aspects of the basic building block of print communications. Numerous examples make its lessons obvious and easy to understand.

White, Jan V., **Editing by Design: A Guide to Effective Word-and-Picture Communication for Editors and Designers**, R. R. Bowker, New York, NY, 1982.

A classic text, **Editing by Design** underscores the importance of a "form-follows-function" approach to graphic design. A great deal of emphasis is placed on integrating photographs and artwork into a finished publication.

White, Jan V., **Mastering Graphics: Design and Production Made Easy**, R. R. Bowker, New York, NY, 1983.

Mastering Graphics elaborates on the ideas first expressed in **Editing by Design**. Although written in pre-desktop-publishing days, it includes numerous "do-it-yourself" applications examples. It's hard not to be excited or motivated by the way the illustrations relate theory to reality.

White, Jan V., **Designing for Magazines: Common Problems, Realistic Solutions**, R. R. Bowker, New York, NY, 1982.

Designing for Magazines uses numerous "before" and "after" examples to illustrate how basic design principles can be applied to the component parts of a magazine: masthead, logo, body copy and illustrations.

White, Jan V., **18 Ready To Use Grids for Standard and 8 1/2" x 11" pages,** National Composition Service, Arlington, VA.

This short publication, available direct from the National Composition Service (1730 North Lynn Street, Arlington, VA 22209), illustrates the diversity of text and photo placement made possible by utilizing the grid system to its fullest. Following a short introduction, the booklet consists of left-hand pages which show the grid full-size, facing right-hand pages which illustrate the different ways the grid can be utilized. Column widths and gutter dimensions are clearly illustrated.

Zinsser, William, **On Writing Well,** Harper & Row, New York, NY, 1985

Another excellent companion for the desktop publisher, **On Writing Well** helps the desktop publisher overcome writer's block and allow ideas to flow in a simple, straightforward fashion.

Zinsser, William. **Writing with a Word Processor,** Harper & Row, New York, NY, 1983.

Writing with a Word Processor shows how an established "traditionalist" shifted his allegiance (and comfort level) from typewriter to CRT screen and floppy disks. Entertainingly written and especially recommended for those new to desktop publishing.

Magazines

The Colophon, Adobe Corporation, Palo Alto, CA.

The Colophon is sent free of charge to interested parties, as well as registered users of the Adobe Illustrator drawing program and registered users of Adobe's downloadable typefaces. Its large format design balances technical "how-to" tips with whimsical treatment of typography-related issues.

Communication Arts, Coyne & Blanchard, Palo Alto, CA. Eight issues/yr.

Communication Arts is best known for its special focus issues which showcase the year's best design entries in various categories, including advertising, illustration, design and photography.

PC Publishing, Hunter Publications, Des Plains, IL. Monthly.

Produced entirely using desktop publishing techniques, this monthly publication features a great deal of buying information, as well as tips and tricks for the novice.

Personal Publishing, Renegade Publications, Itasca, IL. Monthly.

Personal Publishing offers a "hands-on" approach to desktop publishing. It provides practical advice and examples of attainable goals for the self-publisher.

Print: America's Graphic Design Magazine, RC Publications, New York, NY. Bi-monthly.

Print is a large format publication which showcases the latest trends in publication design and production. Emphasis is placed on the careers and design philosophies of practicing designers. Its "Regional Design" issue is notable for highlighting geographic trends.

Publish! PCW Communications, San Francisco, CA. Monthly.

Publish! is a lavish publication featuring the latest hardware and software, as well as profiles of leading desktop publishers around the country. Also included are "How-to!" articles and publication makeovers.

TypeWorld, Typeworld Publications, Salem, NH. Monthly.

Hardware-oriented, **TypeWorld** focuses on the technical aspects of electronic publishing and various facets of the interface between personal computers and phototypesetting equipment.

U & LC, International Typographic Corporation, New York, NY. Monthly.

Although **U & LC** has its basis in traditional phototypesetting, it was among the first to herald the advances made possible by computer-based publishing. Its informal writing style balances its extremely detailed treatment of the latest technical aspects of typography.

Associations and User Groups

MicroSoft Word Users Groups
Roger Shanafelt
Microsoft Corporation
16011 NE 36th Way
Box 9707
Redmond, WA 98073-9717

National Association of Desktop Publishers
P.O. Box 508, Kenmore Station
Boston, MA 02215-9998

Newsletter Association
1401 Wilson Blvd, Suite 403
Arlington, VA 22209

The Newsletter Clearinghouse
44 West Market Street
Rhinebeck, NY 12572

PageMaker Users Groups
Rita Brzusek
Aldus Corporation
411 First Avenue South
Suite 200
Seattle, WA 98104

WordPerfect Support Group
P.O. Box 1577
Baltimore, MD 21203

Ventura Publisher User's Group
16160 Caputo Drive
Morgan Hill, CA 95037

Seminars and Workshops

Dynamic Graphics & Education Foundation
6000 North Forest Park Drive
P.O. Box 1901
Peoria, IL 61656-1901

Three-day hands-on workshops on "Designing for Desktop Publishing," "Basic Layout and Pasteup," "Typography in Design," "Publication Design," "Color in Design and Reproduction," more.

Electronic Directions
21 East Fourth Street
New York, NY 10003

Software-specific courses and seminars on "Ventura Publisher," "PC Pagemaker," "Using Ready, Set, Go!," "Using Quark Xpress," "Using Adobe Illustrator," "PostScript for Designers," "Document Preparation for Linotronic Output," "Basic Typography for Desktop Publishing," "Making Effective Presentations Using Your Personal Computer."

Performance Seminar Group
204 Strawberry Hill Avenue
Norwalk, CT 06851

This group offers one-day seminars on "Designing Effective Newsletters," "How to Buy Printing and Related Services," "How to Write and Design Sales Literature," more.

Promotion Perspectives
1955 Pauline Boulevard, Suite 100A
Ann Arbor, MI 48103

Promotional Perspectives presents several seminars around the country, including: "Newsletter Editing, Design and Production" and "Fundamentals of Design for Desktop Publishing." Participants receive an unusually complete set of working tools and hand-out materials.

Credits

Pages 10 & 11
Mark Sparshott
PhotoResolutions
Denver, CO

Pages 96, 97, 99, 100, 110, 111
Originals and makeovers provided by
Promotion Perspectives
Ann Arbor, MI

Index

Index

Index

Index

To help us improve the quality of our publications...

...we'd appreciate you taking three minutes of your time to complete the survey below.

When you send a completed form to us, we'll add your name to our mailing list, which will keep you informed about upcoming desktop publishing and graphic design books produced by Ventana Press. And we'll enter your name in a drawing for a free two-day workshop on desktop publishing design!

Before reading this book, how much graphic design experience did you have?
1   A good deal
2   Not very much
3   None at all

How important do you feel a knowledge of graphic design is to your desktop publishing productivity?
1   Very important
2   Somewhat important
3   Not important

For what purpose do you use your desktop publishing system? (Circle all that apply.)

1   Brochures
2   User manuals
3   Newsletter
4   Business reports

6   Annual reports
7   Newspaper
8   Magazine
9   Everyday correspondence

5   Other (please specify) _____

What kind of hardware are you using?

1   Apple Macintosh or compatible
2   Atari or compatible
3   Commodore Amiga or compatible

4   IBM or compatible
5   Other (please specify)

_____

6   None yet

What kind of page layout software are you using?

1 Aldus PageMaker
2 GEM Desktop Publisher
3 Quark Xpress
4 Xerox Ventura Publisher

5 Other (please specify)

_____

6 None yet

What kind of graphics or paint software are you using?

1 Adobe Illustrator
2 MacPaint

3 Other (please specify)

_____

4 None yet

What kind of word processing software are you using?

1 Apple MacWrite
2 MicroSoft Word
3 Multimate
4 WordPerfect

5 Wordstar
6 Other (please specify)

_____

7 None yet

How helpful was this book in your work?

1 Very helpful
2 Somewhat helpful
3 Not helpful at all

Please feel free to make any additional comments. We're particularly interested in new books you'd like to see on desktop publishing and design, as well as any suggestions for improving future editions of *Looking Good in Print*.

We appreciate your assistance and wish you success in using your desktop publishing system.

Your Name _____

Firm _____

Street Address _____

City _____ St _____ Zip _____

Telephone Number _____ / _____

Please fold and return to:
Ventana Press, P.O. Box 2468, Chapel Hill, NC 27514

To help us improve the quality of our publications...

...we'd appreciate you taking three minutes of your time to complete the survey below.

When you send a completed form to us, we'll add your name to our mailing list, which will keep you informed about upcoming desktop publishing and graphic design books produced by Ventana Press. And we'll enter your name in a drawing for a free two-day workshop on desktop publishing design!

Before reading this book, how much graphic design experience did you have?
1 A good deal
2 Not very much
3 None at all

How important do you feel a knowledge of graphic design is to your desktop publishing productivity?
1 Very important
2 Somewhat important
3 Not important

For what purpose do you use your desktop publishing system? (Circle all that apply.)

1 Brochures	6 Annual reports
2 User manuals	7 Newspaper
3 Newsletter	8 Magazine
4 Business reports	9 Everyday correspondence

5 Other (please specify) _____

What kind of hardware are you using?

1 Apple Macintosh or compatible	4 IBM or compatible
2 Atari or compatible	5 Other (please specify)
3 Commodore Amiga or compatible	_____
	6 None yet

What kind of page layout software are you using?

1 Aldus PageMaker
2 GEM Desktop Publisher
3 Quark Xpress
4 Xerox Ventura Publisher

5 Other (please specify)
_____
6 None yet

What kind of graphics or paint software are you using?

1 Adobe Illustrator
2 MacPaint

3 Other (please specify)
_____
4 None yet

What kind of word processing software are you using?

1 Apple MacWrite
2 MicroSoft Word
3 Multimate
4 WordPerfect

5 Wordstar
6 Other (please specify)
_____
7 None yet

How helpful was this book in your work?

1 Very helpful
2 Somewhat helpful
3 Not helpful at all

Please feel free to make any additional comments. We're particularly interested in new books you'd like to see on desktop publishing and design, as well as any suggestions for improving future editions of *Looking Good in Print*.

We appreciate your assistance and wish you success in using your desktop publishing system.

Your Name _____

Firm_____

Street Address_____

City_____ St_____ Zip_____

Telephone Number_____ /_____

Please fold and return to:
Ventana Press, P.O. Box 2468, Chapel Hill, NC 27514

Please send me _____ additional copies of Looking Good in Print, at $23.95 per book. Add $3.60 for normal shipping, $5.00 for UPS "two-day air." NC residents add 5% sales tax. Immediate shipment guaranteed.

Note: 15% discount for purchases of 5-9 books. 20% discount for purchases of 10 or more books. Resellers please call for wholesale discount information.

Name _____ Firm _____

Address (no P.O. Box) _____

City _____ State _____ Zip _____

Telephone _____

___Payment enclosed (check or money order; no cash please)

VISA Acc't # _____ MC Acc't # _____

Exp. Date _____ Signature _____

Ventana Press, P.O. Box 2468, Chapel Hill, NC 27515   919/942-0220

Please send me _____ additional copies of Looking Good in Print, at $23.95 per book. Add $3.60 for normal shipping, $5.00 for UPS "two-day air." NC residents add 5% sales tax. Immediate shipment guaranteed.

Note: 15% discount for purchases of 5-9 books. 20% discount for purchases of 10 or more books. Resellers please call for wholesale discount information.

Name _____ Firm _____

Address (no P.O. Box) _____

City _____ State _____ Zip _____

Telephone _____

___Payment enclosed (check or money order; no cash please)

VISA Acc't # _____ MC Acc't # _____

Exp. Date _____ Signature _____

Ventana Press, P.O. Box 2468, Chapel Hill, NC 27515   919/942-0220

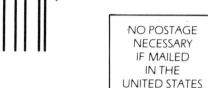

BUSINESS REPLY MAIL

FIRST CLASS MAIL   PERMIT #495   CHAPEL HILL, NC

POSTAGE WILL BE PAID BY ADDRESSEE

Ventana Press

P.O. Box 2468

Chapel Hill, NC 27515

NO POSTAGE
NECESSARY
IF MAILED
IN THE
UNITED STATES

BUSINESS REPLY MAIL

FIRST CLASS MAIL   PERMIT #495   CHAPEL HILL, NC

POSTAGE WILL BE PAID BY ADDRESSEE

Ventana Press

P.O. Box 2468

Chapel Hill, NC 27515

NO POSTAGE
NECESSARY
IF MAILED
IN THE
UNITED STATES

Please send me _____ additional copies of Looking Good in Print, at $23.95 per book. Add $3.60 for normal shipping, $5.00 for UPS "two-day air." NC residents add 5% sales tax. Immediate shipment guaranteed.

Note: 15% discount for purchases of 5-9 books. 20% discount for purchases of 10 or more books. Resellers please call for wholesale discount information.

Name _____ Firm _____

Address (no P.O. Box) _____

City _____ State _____ Zip _____

Telephone _____

___Payment enclosed (check or money order; no cash please)

VISA Acc't # _____ MC Acc't # _____

Exp. Date _____ Signature _____

Ventana Press, P.O. Box 2468, Chapel Hill, NC 27515   919/942-0220

Please send me _____ additional copies of Looking Good in Print, at $23.95 per book. Add $3.60 for normal shipping, $5.00 for UPS "two-day air." NC residents add 5% sales tax. Immediate shipment guaranteed.

Note: 15% discount for purchases of 5-9 books. 20% discount for purchases of 10 or more books. Resellers please call for wholesale discount information.

Name _____ Firm _____

Address (no P.O. Box) _____

City _____ State _____ Zip _____

Telephone _____

___Payment enclosed (check or money order; no cash please)

VISA Acc't # _____ MC Acc't # _____

Exp. Date _____ Signature _____

Ventana Press, P.O. Box 2468, Chapel Hill, NC 27515   919/942-0220

BUSINESS REPLY MAIL

FIRST CLASS MAIL   PERMIT #495   CHAPEL HILL, NC

POSTAGE WILL BE PAID BY ADDRESSEE

Ventana Press

P.O. Box 2468

Chapel Hill, NC 27515

NO POSTAGE
NECESSARY
IF MAILED
IN THE
UNITED STATES

BUSINESS REPLY MAIL

FIRST CLASS MAIL   PERMIT #495   CHAPEL HILL, NC

POSTAGE WILL BE PAID BY ADDRESSEE

Ventana Press

P.O. Box 2468

Chapel Hill, NC 27515

NO POSTAGE
NECESSARY
IF MAILED
IN THE
UNITED STATES